Pony Care

Charlotte Popescu is the eldest daughter of Christine
Pullein-Thompson, well-known author of many popular pony books,
and has been surrounded by horses and ponies all her life. She has
also published two *Horse and Pony Quiz Books* in Armada, the first
of which she began to write when she was fourteen. She has a roan
mare of her own called Rum, and lives in Oxfordshire with her
parents, sister and two brothers. Apart from riding, and animals in
general, her interests include the theatre, travelling and reading.

also in Armada by Charlotte Popescu

ARMADA HORSE & PONY QUIZ BOOKS Nos. 1 & 2
and
GOOD RIDING *by Christine Pullein-Thompson*

PONY CARE
from A-Z

Charlotte Popescu

Illustrated by Christine Bousfield

AN ORIGINAL ARMADA

Pony Care From A-Z was first published
in Armada in 1975 by Wm Collins Sons & Co Ltd
14 St James's Place, London SW1A 1PF

© Charlotte Popescu 1975

Made and printed in Great Britain by
William Collins Sons & Co Ltd Glasgow

INTRODUCTION

If you are already a horse expert, then you won't need this book. But if you're not sure of the difference between linseed and oats – and whether to boil the oats or crush the linseed – or don't know what a girth gall looks like, then it's meant for you. It isn't intended to be a horse-owner's Bible, or a comprehensive horse encyclopaedia – those sort of books already exist in large, thick volumes. But I hope you will find in here the answers to all your questions about looking after a pony and keeping him healthy and happy.

Common sense goes a long way in pony care, but if you are ever unsure about treating a pony's ailments, you should always call a vet or get an expert to advise you rather than try and cure him by yourself. However, let's hope that these occasions may be very few and far between, and that the more you learn about horses and their needs, the more fun you will have looking after them. And I hope this book will help you in finding out how much fun that can be.

Charlotte Popescu

AGE

Age can be told by a horse's teeth and general appearance. The length of a horse's life varies, but the life-span is about twenty-eight years. The oldest known horse whose age was recorded lived for fifty-two years. Horses under four years should not normally be ridden (with the exception of horses which are especially bred and reared for racing young). Horses over twenty should be ridden with extra care and consideration. (see *Teeth*)

young horse   *old horse*

AGED

A horse is said to be aged when seven or over by some experts. But more often 'aged' is used to describe a horse of fifteen years or over when it becomes impossible to judge his age accurately. (see *Teeth*)

ANIMALINTEX

A veterinary poultice sometimes used with an oiled skin over it. (see *Poultices*)

Anti-cast Roller (see *Clothing*)

Anti-sweat Rug (see *Rugs*)

Anvil (see *Shoeing Tools*)

APPROACHING A HORSE

Warn a horse of your approach by speaking to him, calling him by name if you know it. Approach him from the front quietly and without undue haste. Pat him on the neck when you are near enough. Never rush at a horse and never wave a stick, rope or anything else in his face.

AZOTURIA

Usually occurs in very fit, stabled horses which have been rested without having their hard feed (oats, etc.) reduced sufficiently. It is a very distressing complaint. The horse will stop suddenly, sweating and trembling. His hindquarters will stiffen and he may drag his hind legs. He will be in great pain. A vet must be called immediately. All hard food should be greatly reduced or not fed at all. Because Azoturia is liable to reoccur, great care must be taken in future feeding. Azoturia is sometimes called Monday Morning Disease because in the past it often occurred on Mondays when most horses rested on Sundays. Horses living out in several acres rarely get Azoturia as they are able to exercise themselves.

Balding Girth (see *Girth, Balding*)

BALL, MEDICINE
Medicine given to the horse in the form of a ball. Often used in the past as a worm dose or to cure a cough. When giving to the horse the tongue must be held and the ball put as far back in the mouth as possible. A balling gun can also be used. Medicine balls are rarely used nowadays.

BALLING
Balls of snow caking inside a horse's hoof making it impossible to ride. In winter this can be avoided by greasing the soles of the feet.

BANDAGES
It is important that all bandages are properly adjusted.

EXERCISE BANDAGES. Bandages used for exercise and to support weak tendons while at work. About three inches wide, they are usually made of crepe or stockinette. They should cover the leg from below the knee to just above the fetlock joint, with the tapes tied on the outside of the leg. The knot should not come at the front where it can press on the bone or at the back where it can press on the tendon. They should be firmly adjusted over cotton wool or gamgee and, for eventing, are often sewn together rather than tied, or sometimes fastened with special clips. Ponies rarely need exercise bandages.

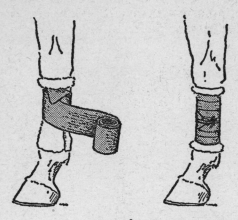

exercise bandages

STABLE BANDAGES. Made of wool or flannel and about four inches wide, these can be worn with or without gamgee underneath for warmth on a clipped horse, or for protection and warmth when travelling. They start below the knee or hock and go right down over the fetlock to just above the coronet.

10

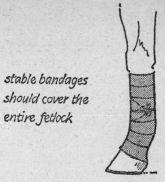

stable bandages should cover the entire fetlock

They are sometimes used loosely attached over straw to dry off wet legs. Long-coated ponies don't need them when stabled, but a horse with clipped legs needs them in winter, when the weather is cold.

TAIL BANDAGE. Usually made of stockinette or crepe and about three inches wide, tail bandages are used to keep a pulled tail tidy. They are also used for protection when travelling by box. Starting at the top of the tail, they should come approximately three quarters of the way down the dock and must be tied on the outside of the tail, (i.e. the bit you

11

see) or they can cause intense irritation. A tail bandage should not be left on for long periods and should never be left on overnight.

Bang Tail (see *Trimming*)

Bar-shoe (see *Shoes, types of*)

Barley (see *Feeds*)

BARS OF MOUTH
Gaps between the tushes and molar teeth where the bit lies in the mouth.

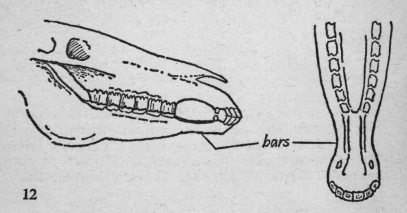

bars

Bars (see *Foot, parts of*)

Bars, Stirrup (see *Saddle*)

Bay (see *Colours*)

Beans (see *Feeds*)

BEDDING

This must be provided if a horse stays in a stable more than a few hours. It should be thick enough to cover the floor entirely and be piled up high around the sides of the box. It is used to encourage a horse to lie down, to protect him from a hard floor and to keep him warm.

STRAW. Wheat straw makes the best bedding. Oat and barley can be used, though barley tends to be prickly and oat tends to be eaten! Straw makes a very comfortable bed and looks lovely, but it needs storage space to keep it if used regularly. Sometimes straw stable manure can be sold to mushroom growers which often pays for the initial cost of the straw. A large bale of straw weighs between 70 and 90 lbs, and you will need more than one to bed down a large box.

SHAVINGS. A comfortable bedding which can be used with or without sawdust. You may be able to buy them cheaply from your local timber merchant or sawmill, but always look carefully for any sharp bits of wood among them or, worse still, nails. If used with sawdust, the sawdust is put down first. Refuse and manure from shavings are usually burnt.

SAWDUST. This makes a comfortable bedding, but tends to clog up drains. Like shavings, it can probably be bought from your local sawmill or timber merchant but should be fresh and dry when bought. You need nearly 3 cwt. of sawdust to make a reasonable bed and about another 1 cwt. a month to

13

a well-bedded loose box

keep it in good condition. If you muck out efficiently you need not renew the whole bed more than once every three months.

PEAT MOSS. Peat moss makes a good bedding but the bed must be kept clean and hoofs picked out regularly. Wet and soiled patches must be removed and the whole bed raked over daily. Soiled peat can be difficult to get rid of and a dirty or damp bed may lead to foot problems.

BISHOPING
A trick to make a horse look younger than he is. A horse's teeth are filed or changed to give them a different appearance. Sometimes when black marks have disappeared they are reproduced by burning with a hot iron.

Biting (see *Vices*)

BITS

Bits come in many shapes and sizes. They are usually made of a type of metal, vulcanite or rubber. Attached to a bridle, they help to keep a horse's head in the correct place. They are also needed for controlling him (i.e. for turning, stopping, regulating pace, etc.). When a bit brings pressure to bear on a horse's mouth, he should relax his jaw. Most snaffles act on the corners of a horse's mouth; other bits often act on the bars of the mouth and the tongue. If used severely these bits do a lot of damage and the horse will either grow frightened of the bit, or develop a hard mouth. Bits need careful fitting; they must neither wrinkle the horse's lips nor come in contact with his teeth. Bits can be divided into several groups (see *Double Bridle*, *Kimblewick*, *Pelham*, *Snaffle*)

Black (see *Colours*)

BLACKSMITH

The blacksmith, sometimes called a farrier, is a man who shoes horses but also does other iron work e.g. making wrought iron gates. He may shoe them at his own forge or travel to the homes of horse owners. (see *Shoeing*)

BLANKET

Woollen blankets are often worn under night rugs.

Blanket Clip (see *Clipping*)

BLISTERING

A treatment for various forms of lameness, although nowadays injections are preferred, where blistering ointment is applied to the affected leg to produce severe inflammation, which quickens repair of the tissues.

Blue-eye (Wall eye) (see *Markings*, *Head*)

Body Brush (see *Grooming Tools*)

Bolting (see *Vices*)

BOTS
Bots are not true worms. They occur after eggs have been laid by gad flies on a horse's legs. If he licks his legs or his mouth comes in contact with the eggs they can be transferred to his stomach where they will hatch into bots. If a horse has a great many bots inside him, he will lose condition. Because of this, bot eggs should be removed from the legs with a blunt knife.

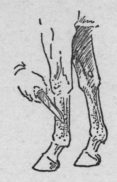

removing bots with a knife

Bran (see *Feeds*)

BRANDING
This is usually done to wild ponies, often foals, so that owners know which are theirs. It is done with a hot iron usually in the form of letters in the saddle area, on the shoulder or the quarters. Occasionally it is done on the hoofs. Branding takes only a few seconds but the marks made will last a pony's lifetime.

16

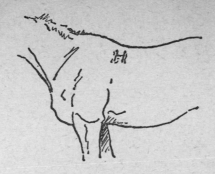

typical brand mark

BREAKING OUT
An unnatural sweating that can be caused by illness, by
nerves or by a horse out of condition, sweating again after
being dried. The horse should be dried again and, if ill, the
vet must be called without delay.

BREAST PLATE (breast piece)
Can be partly made of webbing or entirely of leather. It is
attached to the girth and, with a leather one, to the 'D's' on

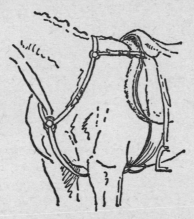

hunting breast plate

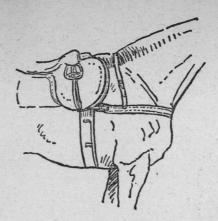

Aintree breast plate

the saddle as well. There are two distinct types. It is used to stop a saddle slipping back.

BRIDLE
Usually made of leather, a bridle is used on a horse's head in conjunction with a bit, to control a horse. A bridle must fit correctly. Bridles come in three main sizes—Pony, Cob or Horse.

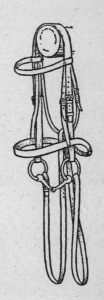

FITTING A BRIDLE. To put the bridle on, approach the near (left) side of the horse and slip the reins over his head. Then holding the top of the bridle with the right hand and the bit in the left hand, gently open the horse's mouth by sliding the left thumb in above the incisors and raise the bit

putting on a bridle

into his mouth, at the same time slipping the headpiece over each ear in turn. Smooth the mane under the headpiece and put the forelock over the browband. Then do up the throat lash making sure your hand can fit between it and the side of the cheek. The noseband must be running inside the cheek-pieces round the horse's nose and should be done up so that three fingers can be fitted between it and the nose. To fit, the bit must lie in the right place in the mouth. It must not be so high that it wrinkles the lips and not so low that it is between the horse's teeth. The height of the bit can be adjusted by the cheek straps which are attached to the headpiece. The bit must also be the correct width. The browband should lie

19

just below the ears but should not press against them. In a double bridle the bridoon must lie immediately above the curb. The curb chain should lie flat in the chin groove and be done up on the near side. The lip strap which holds the chain in position passes through the fly link in the middle of the chain and should not be tight. The various parts of the bridle are as follows:

BROWBAND. A piece of leather which lies in front of the horse's ears across his forehead. It is used to stop the head-piece slipping back and must not be too tight.

CHEEK PIECES. Short straps which attach the headpiece to the bit.

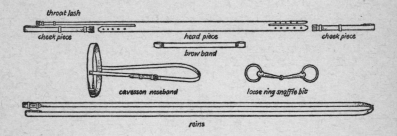

HEADPIECE. This goes over the horse's head behind his ears. The throat lash is attached to it and it goes through two loops at either end of the browband. It is also attached to the cheek pieces.

NOSEBAND (see *Nosebands*).

REINS. The reins are attached to the bit and help to control the horse. They are made of leather, nylon or linen and some-

20

times of plaited leather or rubber-covered leather. They should be the right length and usually have a buckle at the join.

THROAT LASH (latch). This is the part of the headpiece which stops the bridle slipping over the horse's ears. It should never be too tight, or it will affect the horse's breathing.

Bridoon (see *Double Bridle*)

Brisket (see *Points of the Horse*)

BRITTLE HOOF
Cracked and brittle hoofs which easily break, often caused by lack of trimming or bad shoeing. Hoofs should be regularly treated with hoof oil, glycerine or special ointment to encourage growth and then kept in shape by a blacksmith. (see *Sandcrack*)

BROKEN KNEES
Knees scarred or with the flesh broken by stumbling or falling. Newly broken knees should be treated as wounds. But if a horse falls frequently, either he is being ridden badly, his feet are too long and need cutting back, he has weak forelegs,

21

or possibly Navicular is beginning. It is better to avoid buying a horse with badly scarred knees unless you know how they were broken. (see *Navicular, Wounds*)

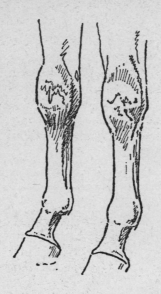

BROKEN WIND
Often caused by riding a horse with a cough or constantly riding after feeding, this is an incurable condition of the lungs. Broken-winded horses will cough if galloped and have difficulty in breathing if ridden fast. Their hay and hard feed should be dampened and they should be used only for slow work or as instructed by a vet.

Browband (see *Bridle, parts of*)

Brown (see *Colours*)

BRUISED SOLE
Usually caused by hitting a stone, the sole will be painful to touch, and possibly red. Treat by shoeing with a piece of leather perhaps covering the entire hoof with a dressing underneath. This can be done by your blacksmith.

BRUSHING (wound)
A wound caused by a horse's hoof hitting another leg when in action, usually the inside of a fetlock but sometimes the coronet. Mostly caused by bad action, faulty shoeing, bad conformation, weakness from old age or weak, feeble riding, i.e. letting your horse go anyhow or driving him at too fast a

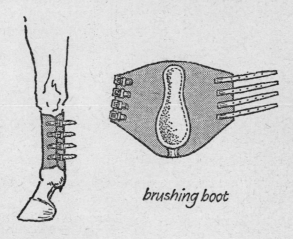

brushing boot

trot so that he becomes unbalanced. A brushing boot will often prevent further trouble, or shoeing with a feather-edged shoe may help. The wound should be treated in the usual way. (see *Shoes, types of, Wounds, Yorkshire boot*)

Buffer (see *Shoeing Tools*)

23

CALKIN (caulkin)

Used much on horses in the past to prevent slipping when pulling heavy loads, a caulkin is the turned down end of a horse's shoe, usually on the hind shoe. It raises the heels but puts added strain elsewhere. Not really recommended, except when prescribed by a vet.

CANNON BONE

The bone which runs from knee to fetlock. It should be short and reasonably wide. If you want to measure bone it is done here below the knee. If the measurement is small a horse may be called 'short of bone' or be 'tied in below the knee'. The cannon bone on the hindlegs is sometimes called the shank. Horses with long cannon bones are more likely to develop strained or sprained tendons than horses with short ones — a point to remember when choosing a horse. (see *Points of the Horse*)

Cantle (see *Saddle*)

CAPPED ELBOW (Shoe-boil)

An enlargement or swelling at the point of the elbow caused by the inner heel of a hind shoe bruising the elbow when a stabled horse is lying down without enough bedding. It can be prevented by a sausage boot, which is a stuffed leather ring put round the coronet. More bedding should be provided without delay. (see *Sausage boot*)

CAPPED HOCK

A swelling at the point of the hock usually caused by a shortage of bedding or a kick. More bedding should be provided and, if it recurs, a hock boot. Massage with lead lotion or call the vet.

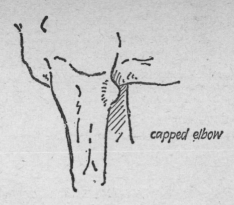

capped elbow

Carrots (see *Feeds*)

CAST
A term used to describe a horse lying down in a stable and unable to get up, either because he is too near a wall or partition or because the stable is too small.

cast against the stable wall

25

CAT HAIRS

Long untidy single hairs which grow sometimes after clipping. They can be removed by singeing. They can also appear on ponies kept out if they are in bad condition or possibly are suffering from worms. (see *Trimming*)

Cavesson (see *Nosebands*)

Chaff (see *Feeds*)

Cheek-piece (see *Bridle, parts of*)

Chest (see *Points of the Horse*)

CHESTNUT

This is a small horny growth found on the inside of all four legs. It is quite natural and should not cause alarm! It grows continually and falls off when too long. It is believed to have been one of the horse's toes in prehistoric times. (see *Points of the Horse*)

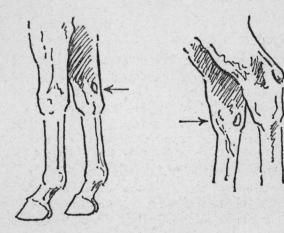

Chestnut (see *Colours*)

Chin Groove (see *Points of the Horse*)

Cleft or Frog (see *Foot, parts of*)

CLENCH
These are the points of the nails that are left sticking out of the hoof when the horse has been shod. They are twisted off and then hammered down to form clenches. (see *Shoeing*).

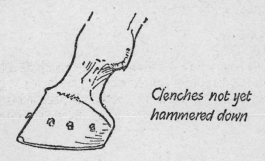

Clenches not yet hammered down

CLIPPING
Done in October and often again in January; a horse is clipped so that he can do fast work without sweating too much and losing condition. This applies particularly to hunting. In olden days before clippers were invented, it was not unusual for horses to die of exhaustion in the hunting field.

Clipping also makes grooming much easier and a clipped horse can be kept much fitter than an animal in his own natural, winter coat. Electric clippers are usually used nowadays, although the old hand-turned machines are still occasionally in use. Clipping requires experience and an assistant may be needed if the horse is nervous. Care must

27

be taken over the head, belly and legs. The inside of ears should never be clipped as this can lead to ear ache. The whiskers round the eyes and nose should never be cut either as these are used as feelers in the dark. A clipped horse, having lost his natural coat, should always be provided with a rug or rugs when not being ridden. A fully clipped horse should never be expected to live out.

TRACE HIGH CLIP. The hair is removed from the belly, underpart of the neck and halfway down the forearm and thighs. This can be done for a pony which lives out provided he has a shelter. He will need to wear a New Zealand rug in really cold or wet weather.

trace high clip

BLANKET CLIP. In this the coat is clipped from head, neck and belly leaving a large patch like a blanket on the horse's back. A horse with a blanket clip can be turned out in a New Zealand rug in the day but needs to be in with a rug at night.

28

blanket clip

HUNTER CLIP. The whole coat is clipped except for the legs and saddle patch. This is a common clip for horses being hunted regularly. Clipped like this, a horse can be turned out in a New Zealand rug on fine days. He will need a rug with a blanket underneath in the stable.

hunter clip

FULL CLIP. Here the whole coat is removed, which makes it easier to look for thorns and cuts on legs and to keep a horse clean. Mainly used on hunters. A fully clipped horse needs to be kept in a rug and blanket at night plus stable bandages on cold nights. Some horses may need two blankets as well as a rug.

CLOTHING (see also *Rugs, Bandages*)

HOCK BOOTS. A covering of padded leather to protect the hocks when travelling.

KNEE CAPS. A covering, usually of felt, to protect the knees when travelling. Two straps fasten the pad of felt above and below the knee. Knee caps are often used on valuable horses when being exercised for protection against injury. The lower strap should always be fitted loosely to allow flexion at the knees.

ROLLER. A kind of girth used to keep a rug in place. A roller is made of leather, webbing, or sometimes hemp, and has two padded panels to prevent pressure on either side of the spine. There are various types, one of which is the arched or anti-cast roller. This has a metal arch joining the two pads which helps prevent the horse becoming cast in the stable.

SURCINGLE. A piece of webbing, hemp, or jute about three inches wide which is usually sewn on to a rug to keep it in place. Not to be confused with a roller. Also, a strap which passes over the saddle as a precaution against the saddle slipping or girth breaking. Most commonly used for racing and eventing.

TAIL GUARD. A covering of leather or jute to protect the tail when travelling.

30

CLOTHING

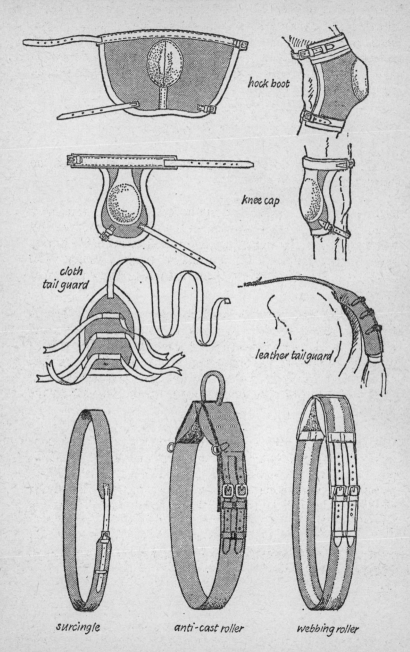

hock boot

knee cap

cloth tail guard

leather tail guard

surcingle

anti-cast roller

webbing roller

COLD

A horse's cold has the same symptoms as the human cold. The horse should be kept warm with plenty of fresh air. He can be fed bran mashes from a bucket on the ground which will help to drain his nostrils. Isolation is excellent if at all possible as this stops the cold spreading. Horses rarely have colds and any cold may be a warning of something more serious, so watch for coughing or for a rise in temperature, when a vet must be called without further delay.

Cold-shoeing (see *Shoeing*)

COLIC (Belly ache, Gripes)

A horse can die of colic and treatment is vital. The symptoms are pawing the ground, kicking at the stomach, sweating, general uneasiness, getting up and down and rolling. It can be caused by faulty feeding causing indigestion, by eating unsuitable substances, by a chill, by drinking a lot of water after eating a feed, by drinking water containing sand, or giving very cold water to a hot horse. Treatment consists of walking a horse up and down so that he cannot roll, keeping him warm, giving a colic drench and by sending for the vet. If you have no colic drench you should send for the vet at once.

The horse must not be left alone because if allowed to roll he may twist a gut which is fatal. If treated in reasonable time, most horses recover from colic without any lasting ill effects.

COLIC DRENCH

Liquid medicine in a thick bottle used to relieve colic. Given by holding up a horse's head and slowly pouring down his throat. An assistant is necessary and a vet should always be sent for if horse is not much better within two hours. It is advisable for the drench to be administered by an expert.

COLOURS

BAY. A bay horse has a black mane, tail and points (limbs). The colour varies from dull red to a yellowish colour. But the most usual bay is the colour of a ripe horse chestnut.

BLACK. A black horse has black pigment throughout the coat except for any white markings. If he has a brown muzzle he is called dark brown.

BROWN. A brown horse's skin contains black and brown pigment so that the coat appears dark brown. The mane, tail and points are also brown. There are light and dark brown horses.

CHESTNUT. A chestnut horse is yellow-coloured. There are three different variations – light, dark and liver chestnut. A dark chestnut has a reddish-coloured pigment. A light chestnut has a more yellowy-coloured coat and a liver chestnut has a more darkly coloured coat. A 'true' chestnut has a chestnut mane and tail. The mane and tail may be darker or lighter than the rest of the body. Lighter chestnuts have flaxen manes and tails but are darker than palominos.

CREAM. A cream horse has a cream-coloured, unpigmented skin. The eye may have a pinkish or bluish tinge.

DUN. A dun horse's colour varies from mouse to golden. The two variations of a dun are blue and yellow. A yellow dun has yellow pigment in his coat but the skin is black. This is the more usual kind of dun. The coat generally turns a dark colour in the winter, but is lighter in the summer. A blue dun has black pigment in his coat and the skin is also black. Sometimes duns have dorsal stripes which run down their backs, often called a donkey stripe. (see *Markings, Other*)

GREY. A grey horse has both black and white pigment in his coat but the skin is black. The coat usually becomes lighter in colour as the horse grows older. Variations of the colour include iron, dappled, light and fleabitten grey. An iron grey horse has a lot of black in his coat and will be a dark colour when young. A dappled grey has a coat of black and white hairs arranged in whorls. In a light grey, white is predominant and in a fleabitten grey dark hair occurs in tufts.

PALOMINO. A palomino has a golden-coloured body with an almost white mane and tail.

PIEBALD. A black and white horse.

ROAN. A roan horse has white hairs mixed with the body colour of chestnut, bay, brown, or black. Variations of the colour are strawberry, bay or blue roan. A strawberry (or sometimes called chestnut) roan shows a pinkish-reddish colour with mane, tail and points the same colour. A bay or red roan is a mixture of bay and white hairs. The limbs, etc. are black. A blue roan has a mixture of black or black-brown and white hairs giving a bluish appearance. The legs from the knee and hock down are black.

SKEWBALD. A skewbald horse has large white patches with other patches of any other colour except black.

ODD-COLOURED. An odd-coloured horse has more than two colours in his coat usually in patches.

34

CONDITION

GOOD. A horse in good condition will be looking his best both in appearance and health. He should be neither too thin, nor too fat and have plenty of hard muscle. His eye should be bright, his skin rippling as he walks, his coat shining. Only good stable management can produce a horse in really good condition. A pony living out needs just the right amount of grass – neither too much, nor too little. Exercise also plays an important part. Too much fast riding makes a horse lose condition very quickly, too little riding can make him soft and flabby.

good condition

BAD. A horse in bad condition can be either too fat or too thin. If his ribs are showing and there are long poverty lines on his quarters, if his neck is poor and drooping and his hoofs cracked, a horse is obviously in very bad condition. An over-fat horse is less obvious, perhaps, but his condition can be dangerous to his health. A huge belly, enormous neck, a

35

horse which puffs and blows even at a trot is obviously too fat and prone to several painful complaints (including some incurable ones if ridden too fast). A very fat horse can be put on a diet; a very thin horse needs a complete overhaul, including a visit from a vet.

bad condition

CORNS
Caused by badly fitting shoes or shoes being left on too long; these appear bluish-red in colour. The shoes must be removed and the foot can be tubbed. Your blacksmith should be consulted and your horse can be shod with a three quarter length shoe if necessary.

Corn, seat of (see *Foot, parts of*)

Coronet (see *Points of the Horse*)

COUGHS
Coughs can be due to indigestion, a cold, something tickling a horse's throat, broken wind, teething, or influenza. If a horse keeps coughing even when standing still, it is not likely to be broken wind, or something tickling his throat and a vet

should be called. Dusty or musty hay can aggravate a cough and a coughing horse should have his food dampened and be kept warm. A horse which coughs and is sweating is obviously ill and a vet must be called at once. At no time should a coughing horse be ridden, nor should he be taken among other horses. This does not apply to horses affected in the wind which are not infectious and may be ridden quietly.

CRACKED HEELS
Chapped and sore heels often caused by horses standing in mud, particularly in winter. Stabled horses can get it, if heels are not properly dried after washing, or if left wet and muddy after hunting. Sometimes lead lotion bandages are applied, or if the condition is mild you can try human remedies, but calling the vet is the best action if the cracks are at all deep.

CRADLE
This is used around the horse's neck so that a sick horse cannot interfere with areas of its body which should be left alone. The cradle consists of round lengths of wood fastened by leather straps to form a device which goes round the neck from throat to shoulder.

Cream (see *Colours*)

Crib-biting (see *Vices*)

Croup (see *Points of the Horse*)

CRUPPER
A leather strap running from under a horse's dock to a 'D' specially provided on the cantle of a saddle. Fat round ponies need a crupper to stop a saddle slipping over their ears when being ridden downhill, so do some ponies with very straight shoulders and short necks. Horses seldom need a crupper as they have better fronts.

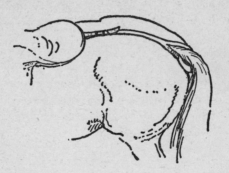

Cubes (see *Feeds*)

CURB
A sprain of the ligament just below the point of the hock at the back. It is caused by a strain. Special treatment is needed e.g. firing, wedged-shaped shoes. Call the vet. (see *Lameness, seats of*)

Curb Bit (see *Double Bridle*)

Curry Comb (see *Grooming tools*)

38

'D' RINGS

These are metal pieces, in the shape of a 'D', built into the saddle to which other pieces of tack, or equipment, may be attached.

Dandy Brush (see *Grooming Tools*)

DISHING

This is a fault in action. The forelegs are thrown outwards as well as forwards when the horse is moving. It is particularly noticeable at the trot.

DOCK

The part of the tail where the hair grows. Less than fifty years ago horses were still having their tails cut off to save work and because they sometimes became entangled in the reins in harness. It was also fashionable at one time. Often the tail was simply chopped off with a chopper, bleeding being stopped by a hot iron. This was called docking. Nowadays the practise is illegal. (see *Points of the Horse*)

DOER

GOOD. A horse which keeps well covered and in good condition with comparatively little food is known as a good doer.

BAD. A horse which in spite of much care and good feeding never succeeds in looking really fit.

Donkey Stripe (see *Markings, Other*)

Dorsal Stripe (see *Markings, Other*)

DOUBLE BRIDLE

A double bridle has two bits, the bridoon and the curb bit, which are described below. The bridle is used on well-schooled horses and helps the horse to flex his jaw and bend

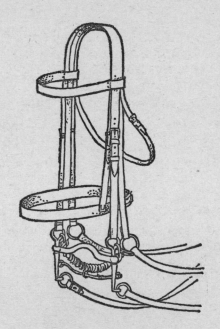

40

his head at the poll. A curb chain is attached to the curb and a lip strap keeps the curb chain in place. Most show hunters and working hunters are shown in a double bridle, so are many high-class show ponies. Very advanced dressage tests are also generally ridden in a double bridle. It is not advisable to use a double bridle unless you are an experienced rider.

BRIDOON. A small jointed snaffle with a thin mouthpiece. This bit should be uppermost in the horse's mouth.

CURB (Weymouth). A bit with a straight mouthpiece, usually with a port, and cheekpieces of varying length. The longer the cheekpiece, the more severe the bit. The action of this bit is on the bars of the mouth and tongue.

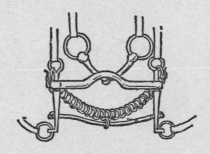

Drawing Knife (see *Shoeing Tools*)

Drench (see *Colic Drench*)

Driving Hammer (see *Shoeing Tools*)

Dropped Noseband (see *Nosebands*)

41

DROPPINGS
These should be regularly removed from the field or scattered. Manure is of great value as a fertiliser and can sometimes be sold either in bags or larger quantities. (see *Manure, Mucking out*)

DUMPING
When a blacksmith shortens the toe by rasping the wall of the hoof in order for it to fit the shoe this is known as dumping. It is a bad practice as the shoe should fit the foot and not vice versa. (see *Shoeing*)

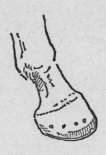

Dun (see *Colours*)

Dung Eating (see *Vices*)

DUTCH SLIP
A small headcollar of leather or webbing usually used on foals.

Eel Stripe (see *Markings, Other*)

Eggbutt (see *Snaffle*)

Elbow (see *Points of the Horse*)

ELECTUARY
A medicine given to horses with coughs and sore throats. It is a paste made basically with treacle and incorporating some drugs. The paste is smeared on the tongue or at the back of the mouth.

ERGOT
A horny growth found at the back of the fetlock joint. It serves no useful purpose and probably dates back to pre-historic times. (see *Points of the Horse*)

Ermine Marks (see *Markings, Legs*)

FARRIER
A man who shoes horses. (see *Blacksmith, Shoeing*)

FEATHER
The hair found on the fetlocks, particularly on Shire Horses and Clydesdales, where it grows long and thick.

Feather-edged Shoe (see *Shoes, Types of*)

FEEDING

Grass is a horse's natural food, but in winter and when working hard, additional food must be provided. Concentrated foods – oats, cubes, nuts, etc. – provide protein and give energy. Hay provides some protein if well made, but is mainly bulk. A small pony can live and work with little besides hay and grass. A well-bred horse needs much more concentrated food. A 14·2 pony will need about 20 lbs. of food a day depending on the type of work, a hunter will need even more – perhaps as much as 12 lbs. of oats a day plus bran, chaff, hay etc. There are some rules which must be followed when feeding.

1. Feed according to the work the horse is doing, i.e. plenty of hard feed for a horse being regularly exercised and hunted. Very little for a horse standing lame in his box, but plenty of hay and green stuff instead.
2. Feed little and often because a horse has a small stomach.
3. Feed plenty of bulk, i.e. hay or grass so that the digestive systems are well used.
4. Feed at the same time every day (if your pony is out and there's some grass, twice a day will do).
5. Never ride after a large feed or when your horse is full of grass or hay as this can ruin his wind. (see *Broken Wind*)
6. Always water before feeding, because a long drink of water can wash food out of the stomach causing illness. A short drink after a feed is all right. (see *Colic*)
7. If your horse is stabled, try to feed something like carrots or chopped apple every day.
8. In winter, feed horses living out as early in the day as you can to prevent them eating frozen grass.
9. Never make sudden changes in your horse's diet – all changes should be gradual. Don't change feeding times suddenly either.

10. Always try to feed good quality food. Buying cheap musty hay is bad for your horse's wind and much will be wasted.

FEEDS

BARLEY. Can be fed either boiled or crushed. Crushed barley can be used to replace oats but is much more fattening and unsuitable for horses doing fast work. Boiled barley is an excellent fattener for horses in bad condition.

BEANS AND PEAS. These are rarely fed nowadays. They are extremely concentrated and must be fed only in small quantities. They must always be split or bruised with a hammer before feeding. A double handful twice a day is more than enough for a pony. They should be mixed with his ordinary feed.

BRAN. This is excellent with oats to provide bulk. It may also be fed dampened as a bran mash.

BRAN MASH. A laxative food which is often fed to a sick horse or after a long day's work. To prepare a bran mash, fill a bucket half or three-quarters full of bran depending on the size of horse and pour boiling water over it until it is all wet but not thin and runny. Put a sack or heavy cloth over it and leave it to steam. Try it on the back of your hand before feeding – it should be nicely warm but not hot enough to burn your horse's mouth. Salt can be added, also a handful of oats, black treacle, or chopped apples and carrots.

CHAFF. Chopped up hay or straw which is often mixed with the feed in order to stop a horse bolting his food. Cut by electric or hand-turned chaff cutter. It also provides bulk.

CUBES, HORSE (pony nuts). A balanced concentrated food consisting of a number of ingredients including oats, barley, bran, maize, grass meal, molasses, minerals and vitamins. The mixture varies depending on what is available at the time of manufacture. Cubes are excellent for very lively horses as they don't make them as excitable as oats, and they can be used to replace oats, $1\frac{1}{2}$ lbs. of cubes having the same feeding value as 1 lb. of oats. They come in different varieties, e.g. Pony cubes and Race Horse cubes. Also Stud cubes which are said to have the most vitamins in them and are fed mainly to foals and brood mares.

GRUEL. This is often fed to horses after a hard day's work. A double handful of oatmeal is placed in a bucket and boiling

FEEDS

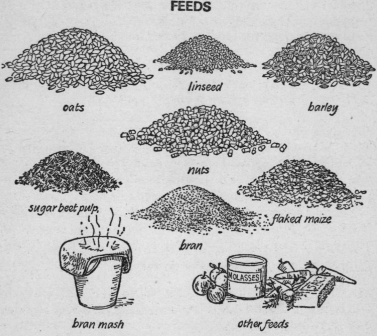

oats

linseed

barley

nuts

sugar beet pulp

bran

flaked maize

bran mash

other feeds

water poured over it. The mixture is then stirred and left to cool. The gruel should be thin enough for a horse to drink.

HAY. Grass of different kinds which is cut and dried and then either stacked and left to mature or, more usually nowadays, baled on the field. It should be cut in late May or June and be greenish-brown in colour, crisp and sweet-smelling. It should not be fed new – the best hay is between six and eighteen months old – because very new hay can give a horse colic. A bale of hay usually weighs between 40 and 56 lbs. but they vary enormously in size. Large rolls of hay are also produced which weigh much more. There are many different kinds of hay, clover being the richest, but not really suitable for horses doing fast work or small, plump ponies. There is also meadow hay from ordinary pasture, sanfoin, timothy, seeded and rye. Sometimes some of these grasses are sown together making an excellent mixture hay. Hay should never be musty, nor black or yellow in colour.

LINSEED. The seed of a flax plant. Linseed is usually fed in winter to improve condition and the appearance of the coat. It may be fed as a jelly, cake, tea or a mash.

LINSEED JELLY. The linseed is soaked in a saucepan of water overnight. Then more water is added and the feed is boiled before being left to cool. The linseed should now be a jelly and is ready to be mixed with the feed.

LINSEED TEA. The tea is made in the same way as the jelly but with more water.

LINSEED CAKE. The linseed is fed dry as nuts or if cake it can be crushed and then added to the feed.

LINSEED MASH. Boiled linseed is added to a bran mash or else water in which linseed has been boiled is added to bran to make a linseed mash.

MAIZE, FLAKED. A nutritious food usually fed with oats to horses in slow work and often used for fattening.

MOLASSES. These are left over after the manufacture of sugar. They are nutritious and help to make a difficult horse accept his feed. They are not commonly fed, are difficult to obtain and expensive.

OATS. The best grain for horses, being easily digested and having great energy value. They may be fed rolled, whole or crushed and should be plump, hard and white or black grains. A hard-working horse may need as much as 14 lbs. daily but a small pony fed too many oats often becomes unmanageable.

ROOTS. Roots such as carrots, swedes, turnips, parsnips, and mangels provide useful succulent food to add to a horse's diet giving bulk and variety. These must always be sliced lengthways and never into round pieces as these may stick in a horse's throat and make him choke.

SUGAR BEET PULP. Nowadays this is a reasonably cheap feed for horses. A small quantity can be fed mixed with the ordinary feed, but it must be soaked overnight beforehand. A large quantity should never be fed to horses doing fast work.

WHEAT. This is an unsuitable grain and should not be fed.

FEED SHED

A special forage store should be kept to store the horse's feed. The shed should have a strong door and even a lock to prevent the horse from reaching the food. Horses, unlike humans, will go on eating until all the food has been eaten and therefore may cause themselves severe illness. The food should be stored in special bins for protection against rats, etc.

FEET
These are the most important part of the horse and need to be treated with great care. When a horse is thought to be lame one should always examine the feet first as lameness occurs most frequently here. (see *Foot, parts of, Lameness*)

FENCES
Wooden post and rail fences are best. Ordinary wire is often used but barbed wire should never be used as it is dangerous. Hedges and walls are satisfactory if kept well.

Fetlock (see *Points of the Horse*)

Fever in the Feet (see *Laminitis*)

FIELD
A horse needs a field of at least two acres for adequate exercise and food. The field should have some shelter – trees and hedges are better than nothing. It should have a good fence and gate and should be constantly checked for anything that might harm a horse, i.e. poisonous plants, glass, wire, etc. A good water supply is essential. But most necessary of all, any field must have an adequate supply of grass for a horse. A horse or pony at grass must be inspected daily. (see *Shelter, Fence, Gate, Water, Grass*)

FILLET-STRING
A cord attached to the back of summer sheets to prevent them blowing up in the wind.

FENCING

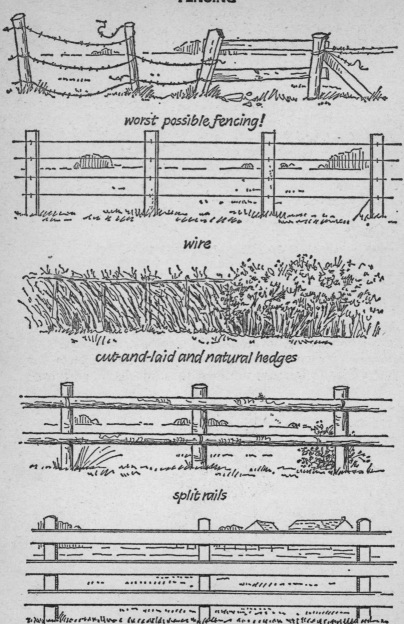

worst possible fencing!

wire

cut-and-laid and natural hedges

split rails

stud rails

FIRING

An operation, usually performed on the front tendons, to help strengthen damaged areas.

Flaked Maize (see *Feeds*)

Flank (see *Points of the Horse*)

Flaps (see *Saddle*)

Flash Noseband (see *Nosebands*)

Flea-Bitten Grey (see *Colours*)

FLECKED

Small white hairs occurring irregularly in the coat.

FLIES

Flies are a great menace to horses in summer. If possible, horses should be brought into a stable in hot weather when flies are at their worst. Anti-fly sprays and ointments specially prepared for horses can also be used though their powers of protection don't usually last more than a few hours. Fly fringes can be fitted to headcollars and special

caps worn. A horse's body can be covered with fly nets and sheets though not when turned out in the field unless properly fixed. All wounds must be protected from flies either with a dressing or fly repellent powder provided by a vet. Horse flies and warble flies should be killed whenever possible as warbles in particular do great damage.

FOMENTATION

This is done to reduce pain and swelling and to bring pus to the surface of infected wounds. The treatment is carried out by soaking a piece of blanket in a bucket of warm water and then applying this to the injured area. The water should never be too hot (if you can soak your hand in it it's hot enough). Cotton wool can be used on a small wound with antiseptic added to the water. On an injured leg, the piece of blanket should be soaked in the water and then wrung out and wrapped round the affected part for a few minutes, removed, put in the water and applied again, and so on for at least twenty minutes. If the foot needs fomenting, an obliging horse will often stand in a bucket of warm water; otherwise you must hold a hot wad of blanket to his hoof or wrap it round as for a limb, depending on the part which needs fomenting. (see *Kaolin, Poultices*)

FOOT, PARTS OF (see opposite)

Fore-arm (see *Points of the Horse*)

FOREHAND

The head, neck, forelegs, shoulders and withers of the horse are collectively known as the forehand.

Forelock (see *Points of the Horse*)
52

THE FOOT

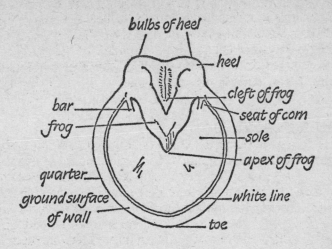

bulbs of heel

heel

cleft of frog

seat of corn

sole

apex of frog

bar

frog

white line

quarter

ground surface of wall

toe

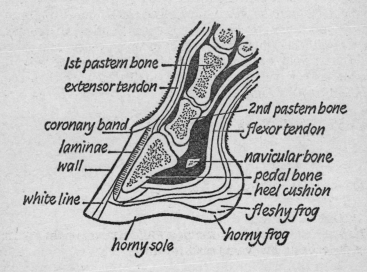

1st pastern bone

extensor tendon

coronary band

laminae

wall

white line

2nd pastern bone

flexor tendon

navicular bone

pedal bone

heel cushion

fleshy frog

horny frog

horny sole

FORGING

This occurs when a hind shoe hits the front shoe while a horse is trotting. A distinct clicking sound is heard as the shoes collide. Forging may occur because the horse is young, green, or when he is tired, or simply when ridden badly. To prevent forging, the fore shoes should be made concave on the inside and the hind shoes should be flat and thinnest at the heel.

Fork (see *Stable Tools*)

Founder (see *Laminitis*)

FRESH

A word given to a horse that is alert and excitable.

a fresh pony will shy at strange objects

FROG

A part of the foot which forms a V shape in the sole. On contact with the ground it provides an anti-slipping device and acts as a shock absorber for the leg. It is very important to keep this part of the foot in good condition. (see *Foot, parts of*)

Frost Nails (see *Studs*)

Full Clip (see *Clipping*)

FULL MOUTH
A horse is said to have a full mouth at six years old.

Full Panel (see *Saddle*)

FULLERING
A groove in the bottom of the shoe in which the nail holes are placed. This groove provides the horse with a better grip on the ground. (see *Shoes*)

GALLS
GIRTH GALL. An abrasion of the skin behind the elbow. Girth galls occur on ponies in soft condition, but also as a result of too tight, too loose or a badly-adjusted girth. Dirty girths also often cause galls. The galls should be cleaned and an ointment used to reduce swelling. Salt and water can be used to harden the skin when the gall has healed. A balding girth can be tried if it won't touch the sore parts, but it is best not to use a saddle until the gall has healed.

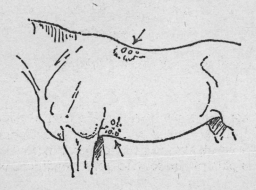

SADDLE GALL (Saddle sore). An abrasion of the skin on the back in the saddle area. The causes are usually pressure from a badly-fitting saddle which can pinch the withers or a saddle which needs restuffing or has a broken tree. Other causes may be bad and unbalanced riding or too much riding on a soft or unfit horse. Treat by applying kaolin paste and hardening the skin with salt and water. A horse can be ridden in this condition using a numnah under the saddle with a hole cut in it over the gall to relieve pressure.

GALVAYNE GROOVE (*Galvayne Mark*)

A groove which appears on the corner incisor teeth when the horse is about nine or ten years and disappears at the age of about twenty. (see *Teeth*)

GAMGEE

A kind of cotton wool that is used under bandages on the legs for exercise and also sometimes under stable bandages.

Gaskin (Second Thigh). (see *Points of the Horse*)

GATE

The gate of a horse's field should be wide, shut well and have a suitable catch. A wooden gate is often used in the show ring for jumping when it is usually five-barred.

56

GIRTH

A strap of nylon, webbing, leather or string which goes under the belly and keeps the saddle in place. Clean, soft leather girths are the best type but are inclined to slip. String girths do not last as long as leather girths and often stretch when first used. Webbing girths tend to create girth galls and sometimes break, so two should always be used when hunting. Nylon girths are commonly used. (see *Tack cleaning*)

GIRTHS

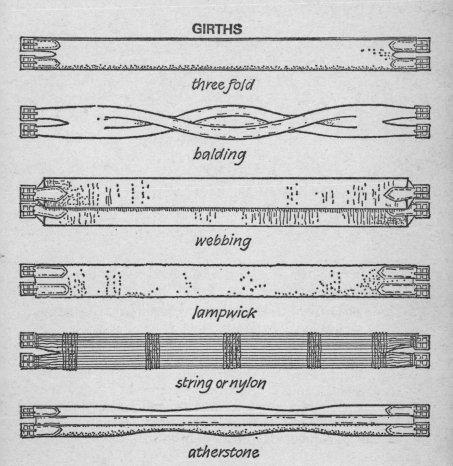

three fold

balding

webbing

lampwick

string or nylon

atherstone

GIRTH, BALDING
A special girth that prevents girth galls. The girth is plaited, being split into three leather straps.

Girth Gall (see *Galls*)

Girth Straps (see *Saddle*)

GONE IN THE WIND
This means a horse is unsound in wind and is affected by whistling, roaring or broken wind.

Grakle Noseband (see *Nosebands*)

GRASS
Nature's natural perfectly balanced food for a horse. It is most nutritious in spring. In winter it does not grow and hay must be fed. (see *Feeding, Field*)

Grass Tips (see *Shoes, types of*)

Grey (see *Colours*)

Gripes (see *Colic*)

GROOMING
This is an essential procedure in caring for a pony. Its objects are to improve the appearance, keep the skin in good order by preventing disease and to keep the coat clean. It also helps to promote health and keep the horse in good condition. The coat is kept greasy and waterproofed by the oil glands. If a horse is out at grass in winter it is essential for him to maintain enough oil to keep himself warm and therefore a body brush should never be used in the winter. A clipped horse should not be groomed with a dandy brush where his coat has

been removed. When grooming a horse the hoofs should be picked out first. Then, starting at the poll, preferably on the near (left) side, groom first with the dandy brush, then the body brush. Next use the water brush and sponge, followed by the wisp and mane comb. The hoofs should then be oiled and finally the coat given a polish with the stable rubber.

QUARTERING. For a stabled horse this should be carried out first thing in the morning. The feet should be picked out and the sponge used on the eyes, nose and dock. The rugs are not removed but thrown forward or back and the parts are given a quick brush. The horse is now clean for morning exercise.

STRAPPING. A thorough grooming.

SET-FAIR (Brush over). The horse is given a quick brush over before being settled for the night. The stable is bedded down and the horse is made comfortable.

GROOMING TOOLS

BODY BRUSH. A brush of short bristles with a loop of webbing across the back. It is used to remove excess dust and sweat and scurf from the coat and also for brushing a well-groomed mane and tail. It should always be used in conjunction with the curry comb.

CURRY COMB. A tool made of metal or rubber with a wooden handle or loop of webbing, used for scraping the dirt from a body brush. A rubber one may be used for grooming a coat; but not on a clipped or ticklish horse!

DANDY BRUSH. A brush of strong bristles used for removing hard caked dirt from the coat of a pony out at grass.

HOOF PICK. A hooked tool for removing dirt and stones from the horse's feet.

59

GROOMING KIT

rubber currycomb

plastic currycomb

dandy brush

metal
currycomb

water brush

body brush

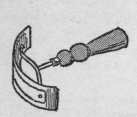

mane comb

stable rubber

hoof pick

wisp

sponge

sweat scraper

MANE COMB. A metal comb used on the mane and sometimes the tail. If used too much it is liable to break or tear out the hair. It is often used when plaiting the mane to separate the hair.

SPONGE. A sponge is used for cleaning the eyes, nose and dock. A separate sponge should be used for the dock.

STABLE RUBBER. A linen cloth used after brushing to give the coat a final polish.

SWEAT SCRAPER. A metal tool with a handle at one end. It is used for scraping sweat from the horse.

WATER BRUSH. A brush with longer bristles than the body brush but otherwise similar to it. The brush is used damp on the mane and tail and sometimes on the legs and feet. It is also used to lay the mane so that it stays on one side.

WISP. A wisp is a twisted rope of hay or straw which is made into a pad. It is used to improve the skin and coat by stimulating circulation and helps form muscle. It also causes the coat to shine by making the glands in the skin produce more oil. A wisp should be used mainly on the neck, thighs and quarters and slapped down smartly on the coat in the direction it lies.

Gruel (see *Feeds*)

Gullet (see *Saddle*)

HACK
To go for a ride across country for pleasure. A horse used for this purpose is also known as a hack. This word originated in the days when riding was mainly a means of transport.

HACKAMORE
The most common form of bitless bridle. It has a single rein and is very severe in use because it acts on the nose and chin. It is of Mexican origin. If wrongly used it could hamper breathing so should be adjusted by an expert.

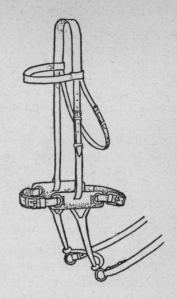

HALTER
A simplified headcollar usually made of hemp, jute or rope used for catching and tying up a horse.

HAM-STRING
A tendon that runs down the thigh of the hind leg. It is the most hard-worked tendon in the horse's body.

HAND
The term used for measuring a horse. A hand equals four inches. The height of a horse is measured at the withers.

HANDLED
A young horse is said to be handled when he can be led in a halter and is accustomed to people being near him.

Hay (see *Feeds*)

HAY-NET
A corded net, often tarred, to hold hay when hung in the stable and also sometimes in the field. Hay-nets are available in three sizes: large (hunter) holding 10-12 lbs. of hay, medium (cob size) holding 7-8 lbs. and small holding 3 lbs. In stables, a hay-net must be tied to a ring at a height not low enough to let the horse catch his foot in it and not high enough to give him neckache or make hay dust fall in his eyes. The hay-net should be secured with a quick-release knot. In the field it should be secured to a strong fence and, as in stables, hung at a sensible height.

HEADCOLLAR (Head Stall)

A form of halter, usually made of leather, but more reliable and better made. A headcollar should have a rope with a quick release fastener.

HEAD SHAKING

This is usually caused by an ill-fitting bridle. The part causing the head shaking should be found and corrected. It can also be caused by bad teeth, ear ache and a variety of other complaints.

HEALTH

Indications of good health are: an alert horse with erect head, bright eyes, pricked ears, shiny, well-conditioned coat, supple skin, eating naturally and producing normal droppings.

Heel (see *Points of the Horse*)

HIND QUARTERS
The area behind the flank including the hind legs.

Hips (see *Points of the Horse*)

Hock (see *Points of the Horse*)

Hock Boot (see *Clothing*)

HOGGING THE MANE
The mane is removed completely with clippers. The mane may be hogged because it is ragged and scruffy or just so that the mane no longer has to be cared for. Hogging has to be repeated every three weeks. It will take approximately two years for the mane to grow out again.

HOOF
The hoof is the horn which covers the outside of the foot from below the coronet. (see *Foot, parts of*)

P.C.—C

HOOF OIL
An oil which should be used on the hoofs to prevent cracking and the hoofs becoming brittle. It is applied with a brush.

Hoof Pick (see *Grooming Tools*)

HORSEFLY
A long-bodied fly which brings irritation to horses. The females suck the animal's blood. They should be killed on sight!

HOSE-PIPING
Water is used from a hose on sprains etc. to reduce swelling and pain and also to clean wounds. Twenty minutes is usually long enough and an assistant may be needed.

Hot Shoeing (see *Shoeing*)

Hunter Clip (see *Clipping*)

Hunter Shoe (see *Shoes, Types of*)

INCISORS
The front teeth which are used for biting. These teeth determine a horse's age. Of the six incisors in each jaw, the two middle teeth are centrals, the next two are laterals and the outside teeth on each side are corners. (see *Teeth*)

INFLUENZA, EQUINE
This is a contagious infection and always involves coughing. There is usually a rise in temperature and coughing lasts for ten days or more. It is now possible for horses to have injections to prevent them catching some influenza viruses, though not all. (see *Coughs*)

Irish Martingale (see *Martingales*)

Iron (see *Stirrups*)

JOCKEYS
Little bits of grease that are found on saddlery. They should be removed.

JUTE RUGS
Night rugs are usually made of jute. (see *Rugs*)

KAOLIN PASTE
A thick paste used on swellings, bruises and other wounds. Before use the tin of paste must be put in a saucepan and boiled for a few minutes. The paste may be used as a poultice. (see *Poultices*)

KEEPER
A leather loop stitched to the various parts of a bridle to keep strap ends in place.

Kicking (see *Vices*)

KIMBLEWICK
A one-rein pelham often used on ponies. The bit has a small port and a curb chain and only having one rein is easier to manage than a pelham or double bridle.

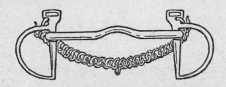

Kineton Noseband (see *Nosebands*)

Knee (see *Points of the Horse*)

Knee Caps (see *Clothing*)

Knee Roll (see *Saddle*)

KOCHOLINE
A kind of grease often used on tack to preserve the leather.

LAMENESS
A lame horse may limp, or hobble or hardly move at all. If the lameness is not severe it may not be evident at the walk but will show at the trot. If your horse is lame, unless there are visible signs of injury, try to discover in which leg he is lame. Find someone to trot him along a hard, flat surface, preferably a road, with his head free from restraint. If you suspect a foreleg, each time the sound leg hits the ground he will nod his head. With a hind leg you will also notice the weight falling on the sound leg. Once the leg is found look for the part which is causing the lameness. Always suspect the foot first because 90% of all lameness occurs here. Look for heat, swelling or painful or tender parts, and then treat the injury in the appropriate way. One of the most common causes of lameness is a stone in the horse's foot, which can easily be removed and then the horse will go sound.

(See *Broken knees, Bruised sole, Brushing, Capped elbow, Capped hock, Corns, Cracked heels, Curb, Laminitis, Nail binding, Navicular, Over-reaching, Pricked foot, Ringbone, Sandcrack, Sidebone, Spavin bog, Spavin bone, Splint, Sprained fetlock, Sprained tendon, Thorough-pin, Thrush, Treads, Wind-gall*).

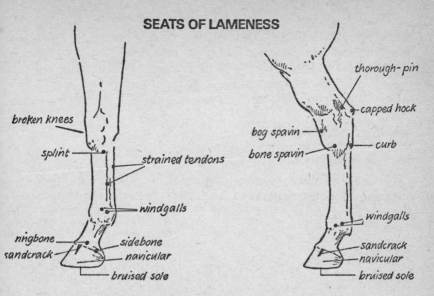

broken knees
splint
strained tendons
windgalls
ringbone
sandcrack
sidebone
navicular
bruised sole

thorough-pin
capped hock
bog spavin
bone spavin
curb
windgalls
sandcrack
navicular
bruised sole

LAMINITIS (Founder, fever in the feet, pony gout)
Nearly always caused by too much spring grass or an excess
of rich grass. This is an extremely painful complaint. The
sensitive laminae under the wall of the feet are affected and
the hoof may feel hot to the touch. A horse with laminitis
may be very or only slightly lame. He will stand on his heels

thrusting his feet forward in front. In a bad case he may not want to move at all and his breathing may be heavy. He must be removed from the grass and a vet should be sent for without delay. Laminitis is a recurring complaint and a pony which has had it should be kept off rich grass in spring and summer months and exercised regularly.

Leathers (see *Stirrups*)

LEATHER PUNCH
This is a tool used for punching holes in leather, e.g. nosebands or stirrup leathers.

LICE
Small grey parasites which suck blood. These are found in winter on long-coated horses behind the ears, in the mane and along the back. The horse may rub bare patches on the crest, shoulders and tail. A parasitic dusting powder will destroy the lice. Equine lice do not affect humans.

Linen (see *Saddle linings*)

Linseed (see *Feeds*)

LIP STRAP
A small leather strap which keeps the curb chain in place. It is attached to the cheeks of the curb bit and is threaded through the fly link on the curb chain.

List (see *Markings, Other*)

LITTER, DEEP
A stabling system whereby only soiled straw is removed and straw is added daily. A very deep bed develops. When the

bed reaches a depth of two feet the whole lot is removed. This system saves work but can cause foot trouble.

LOG
A wooden block with a hole through it, usually used with the headcollar on a horse who is being tied in a stall overnight. The end of the headcollar rope is passed through the block and knotted, giving the horse as much rope as possible.

Loins (see *Points of the Horse*)

Loose Box (see *Stable*)

71

LUNGEING CAVESSON
This is a special kind of noseband used in the training of young horses. It has a padded nosepiece with three rings, to which the lunge rein is attached. (see *Nosebands*)

Maize (see *Feeds*)

Mane (see *Points of the Horse, Trimming*)

Mane Comb (see *Grooming Tools*)

MANGE
A highly infectious skin disease often starting on the head and neck. The horse should be isolated and everything must be disinfected. A vet should be consulted. Fortunately this disease is very rare in the British Isles.

MANGER
Used for feeding horses in the stable. They are usually of iron or wood and should be fitted at breast level with plenty of width and depth. They are often placed in a corner of the stable. They must always be kept clean.

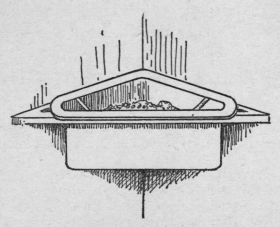

MANURE

The droppings of a horse. The manure heap should be kept tidy in a position near to the stables. Good stable management is often judged by the manure heap. (see *Droppings, Mucking out*)

MARKINGS, HEAD

BLAZE. A broad white marking down the face extending from between the eyes often to the muzzle.

SNIP. A small white marking in the region of the nostrils.

STAR. Any white marking on the forehead.

STRIPE (race). A narrow white marking down the face.

WHITE FACE. A face with white hair covering the forehead, eyes and nose.

WALL-EYE. An eye which has a pinkish-white or bluish-white appearance.

MARKINGS, LEG

ERMINE MARKS. Black spots occurring on a white background.

SOCK. White extending from the coronet and a short way up the leg.

STOCKING. A white leg up to the knee or hock. There is an old saying about white-legged horses. One of the versions is:

> Four white legs keep him not a day,
> Three white legs send him far away,
> Two white legs give him to a friend,
> One white leg keep him to the end. '

MARKINGS

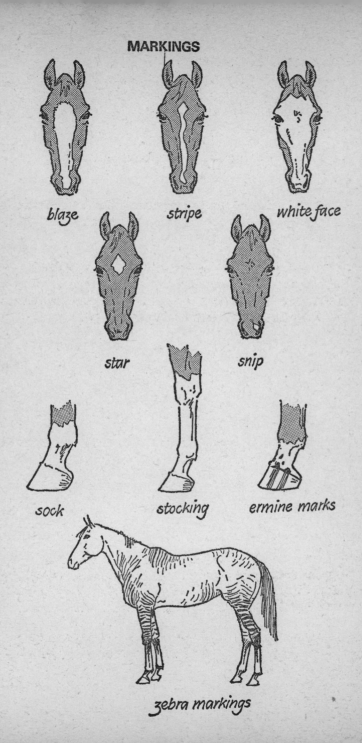

blaze

stripe

white face

star

snip

sock

stocking

ermine marks

zebra markings

MARKINGS, OTHER

DORSAL STRIPE (Donkey or eel stripe, list, ray). A black, brown, or dun stripe extending from the withers to the tail. Typical of Northern and highland breeds and is of ancient origin.

ZEBRA MARKS. Striping on the neck and limbs.

MARTINGALES

These are generally used to regulate a horse's head carriage. Many showjumpers use running martingales. A martingale should never be too tight when jumping.

IRISH MARTINGALE. A leather strap about six inches long with a ring at each end through which the reins are passed beneath the horse's neck. It prevents the reins being thrown over the horse's head and keeps them in place.

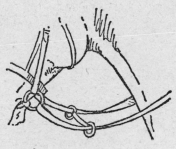

Irish martingale

RUNNING MARTINGALE. A strap with a loop at one end attached to the girth between the front legs. At the other end the strap divides into two, with two rings at the ends, through which the reins are passed. A neck strap supports the martingale. This martingale prevents the head being carried

75

above the angle of control. When the martingale is attached to the girth the straps with rings should reach the withers for a correct fitting. Care should also be taken to see that the rings of the martingale cannot get hooked round the bit rings. This can be prevented by putting rubber stops on the reins.

STANDING MARTINGALE. A strap which runs from the girth to the noseband between the front legs. It is also supported by a neck strap and prevents the horse carrying his head too high. This martingale cannot be used with a dropped noseband. When it is correctly adjusted the horse should not be able to raise his head above the height of the withers.

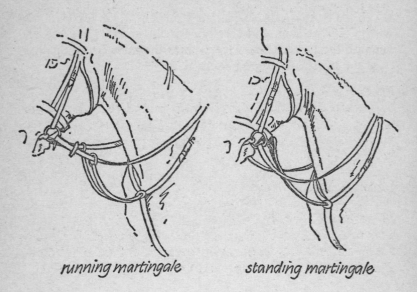

running martingale   standing martingale

Mash (see *Feeds*)

MEALY NOSE
An oatmeal-coloured muzzle. A mealy nose is a characteristic of the Exmoor pony.

76

MEDICINE CUPBOARD

A cupboard should be kept containing essential first aid equipment for your horse. Here is a list of the main items needed:

Disinfectant
Surgical bandage (3 in.)
Scissors
Lint
Cotton wool
Gamgee tissue
Colic drench
Oiled silk (mackintosh)
Boracic powder

Lead lotion
Cough electuary
Kaolin paste
Witch-hazel lotion
Epsom salts
Glycerine
Some eye ointment
A veterinary thermometer

(see *Colic Drench, Electuary, Gamgee, Kaolin Paste*)

MOLARS

These are the back teeth which lie behind the bars of the mouth. They are used for grinding and chewing food. If they become sharp or uneven they will need to be rasped by the vet. (see *Teeth*)

Molasses (see *Feeds*)

MUCKING OUT

The droppings and soiled manure are removed from the stable which is usually swept out every morning and evening. A fork, shovel, broom and wheelbarrow or skip are used.

MUD FEVER

Swellings occurring on the heels and legs caused by mud and wet. Also caused by legs not being dried enough after washing – which removes the natural oil. Treat by applying lead lotion bandages and afterwards boracic powder. In bad cases call the vet without delay.

MUZZLE
A bucket-shaped covering for the nose, either to prevent a horse biting, or eating his bed or his dung. It can be made of leather or net.

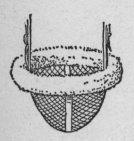  

wire muzzle ·   blocked leather muzzle   open leather muzzle

Muzzle (see *Points of the Horse*)

NAIL-BINDING
Nail binding is when the nail of a shoe is driven too close to the sensitive part of the foot and presses on it. If the nail is removed the horse will go sound.

NAVICULAR
An incurable disease of the navicular bone in the fore-feet. Causes are thought to be mainly concussion (too much hard work after a rest), hereditary weakness or bad shoeing. Symptoms, apart from lameness, are pointing of the toe and stumbling. Special shoes can be used, with rolled toes and thickened at the heel to relieve pressure. It is possible to have the foot de-nerved to relieve pain and lameness, but this is not altogether satisfactory. A horse with straight pasterns or constricted hoofs is more likely to be affected by navicular.

NEAR-SIDE
The left side of the horse.

NEIGH
The call of a horse. From a stallion it often indicates the mating call.

New Zealand Rug (see *Rugs*)

Night Rug (see *Rugs*)

NOSEBAG
A bag used for feeding purposes with a strap round the horse's head keeping the bag in place.

NOSEBANDS
The noseband goes round the horse's nose and is attached to a strap which lies below the head piece. The various kinds of noseband are as follows:

CAVESSON. This noseband can be used with any bridle and only really serves the purpose of providing something on to which to attach a standing martingale. It may also improve the appearance of some horses.

To fit correctly, three fingers should be allowed between the noseband and the horse's nose.

DROPPED NOSEBAND. This noseband can only be used with a snaffle. The front strap is fitted above the nostrils while the back strap passes below the mouthpiece and fits into the chingroove. A dropped noseband prevents the opening of the mouth, crossing of the jaw and getting the tongue over the bit, but needs careful fitting.

79

NOSEBANDS

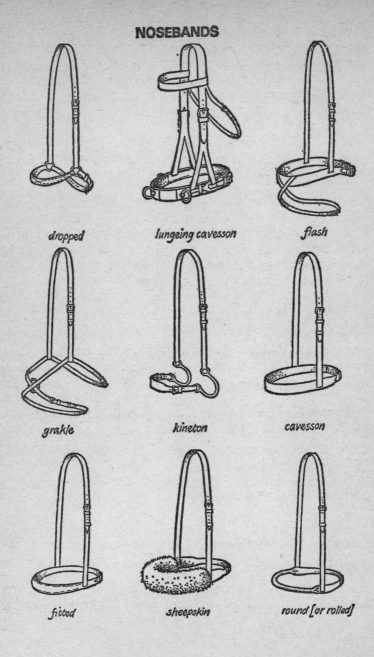

dropped

lungeing cavesson

flash

grakle

kineton

cavesson

fitted

sheepskin

round [or rolled]

FLASH NOSEBAND. An ordinary noseband to which two crossing straps are attached which fasten beneath the bit in the chingroove like a dropped noseband. It is often used when both a standing martingale and a dropped noseband are required.

GRAKLE (double noseband). A crossed noseband which prevents the horse opening his mouth too wide or yawing.

KINETON NOSEBAND (puckle). This noseband has two semi-circles of metal (often leather covered) which fit either side of the mouth behind the bit. Through the action of the bit pressure is brought to bear on the horse's nose. It is useful for a strong pulling horse.

NUMNAH
A pad of felt, sheepskin or rubber cut slightly larger than the shape of a saddle. It is used under a saddle to reduce pressure, usually on a sensitive back and is attached to the saddle by leather straps. It may also be used under a badly-stuffed saddle or with a hole cut in it so that a saddle does not press on a sore back. If used for a long period it may overheat a horse's back. (see *Tack Cleaning*)

Oats (see *Feeds*)

Odd Coloured (see *Colours*)

OFF SIDE
The right side of a horse.

OVER-REACHING
Over-reaching is when the toe of a hind shoe strikes the fore-leg at the heel or higher up. This usually happens at a gallop

or when jumping and should be treated as for a bruised wound with an antiseptic dressing. Over-reach boots can be worn on the forelegs to prevent injury. (see *Wounds*)

PAD SADDLE
This is a special kind of numnah made only of felt. It is carefully adapted for use on small fat ponies. This numnah has no tree and may have a web girth attached.

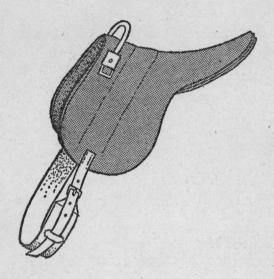

PADDOCK
A smallish area of grazing suitable for the keeping of horses.

Panel (see *Saddle*)

Pastern (see *Points of the Horse*)

Peas (see *Feeds*)

Peat Moss (see *Bedding*)

PELHAM
A bit with a bar mouthpiece and double rings so that two reins are used to give the actions of the curb and bridoon of a double bridle. Occasionally a single rein is attached to a rounding of leather which joins the two rings on the cheek of the bit.

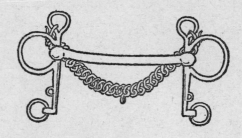

Piebald (see *Colours*)

Pincers (see *Shoeing Tools*)

PIPE-OPENER
A gallop to clear a horse's wind.

Plain Stamped Shoe (see *Shoes, types of*)

PLAITING
Plaits are worn mostly in the show ring to improve the appearance of the neck and smarten the horse. Plaiting is also helpful to train the mane to fall on the correct side of the neck, which is generally accepted to be the off side. There should be an even number of plaits including the forelock and the number usually varies according to the size of neck and mane, but commonly six plaits are made. To plait, a

83

water brush, thread, needle, scissors, and a mane comb are needed. The mane should be dampened, divided into parts, plaited and each plait doubled under. On a thick mane this may have to be done twice. The thread should match the colour of the mane. Rubber bands are sometimes used. (see *Trimming*)

Tail plaiting is generally done to smarten tails that have not been pulled. Tails can also be bound up to keep them clean while out hunting.

POINTS OF THE HORSE

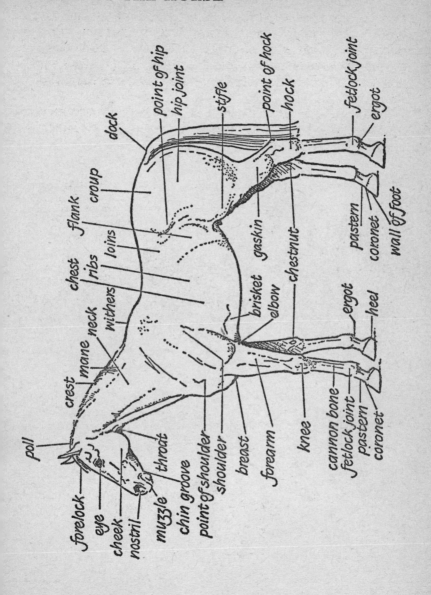

POISONOUS PLANTS

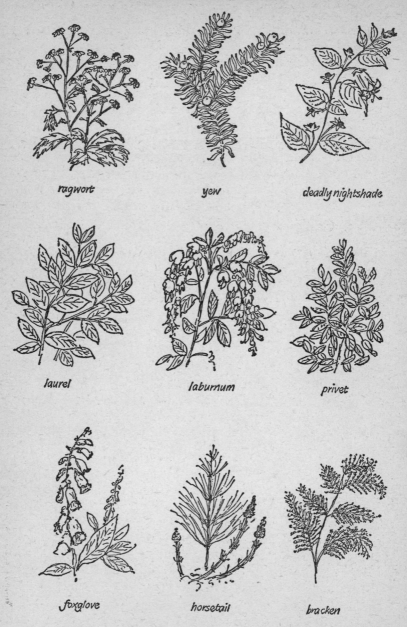

ragwort

yew

deadly nightshade

laurel

laburnum

privet

foxglove

horsetail

bracken

POISONOUS PLANTS

Ragwort, yew and deadly nightshade are all deadly to horses. Ragwort can be recognized by its yellow flower. It may easily be found in fields and should be pulled up and burnt before the plant goes to seed. It should never be pulled up and left as the dead plant is even more dangerous than the living one. Yew trees may be found all over the countryside and the leaves, bark and berries are all poisonous. Deadly nightshade is rare and usually absent from fields. Other not so dangerous plants are laurel, laburnum, and privet. These are slow-poisoning plants. Rarer still are ground ivy, vetches, meadow saffron, bluebells, horsetails, fox gloves, and coniferous trees which can be harmful if eaten in quantity. Bracken and acorns can also be dangerous.

Poll (see *Points of the Horse*)

POLL EVIL

A painful swelling occurring between the ears as a result of a severe blow or pressure from a headcollar. Hot fomentations may be helpful but a vet should be consulted. The horse cannot be ridden as his head is painful. Poll evil is often caused by a horse hitting his head on a low doorway.

Pommel (see *Saddle*)

Pony Gout (see *Laminitis*)

PORT

An arch in the centre of the mouthpiece of some bits to give room for the tongue. The larger the indent the severer the bit.

POULTICES

A soothing application put on the infected part of a horse's body either to clean and provide antiseptic for a wound or soothe in cases of bruises, abscesses or swellings. There are various kinds of poultices:

A kaolin poultice is one of the most common. The tin of kaolin paste must be boiled first and after being tested for temperature applied to the wound under cotton wool and oiled skin with a bandage to keep it in place.

Epsom salts and glycerine provide a poultice in the same way under cotton wool and oiled skin.

A bread or bran poultice is made by pouring boiling water on to bread crumbs or bran, covering with a cloth and applying under an oiled skin or waterproof plastic.

Poultices may also be made with linseed or antiphlogistine which is made from clay. Animalintex is a very good veterinary poultice. A sack can be put over poultices on the foot.

PRICKED FOOT
A foot is said to have been pricked when a nail has been driven into the sensitive part. This may cause a punctured wound which will need professional attention.

PRIME AGE
Between the ages of six and ten years a horse is said to be in his prime. (see *Teeth*)

Pritchel (see *Shoeing Tools*)

Puckle (see *Nosebands, Kineton*)

88

PULSE
The normal pulse of a horse is 36 to 40 beats per minute. It is taken from an artery under the jaw or from inside the foreleg.

PUT DOWN
A horse is said to be put down when he is destroyed because of illness, injury or old age. This is usually done by a vet with a humane killer.

Quartering (see *Grooming*)

Quarters (see *Hindquarters*)

QUIDDING
This is caused by faulty teeth. Food is dropped from the horse's mouth while he is chewing it. It is usually caused by sharp teeth. A vet should be called and the teeth rasped.

Racing Plate (see *Shoes, types of*)

RACK-UP
To tie a horse up to a ring in the wall in his stable or outside in the yard, usually when grooming.

RASP
A file used on a horse's teeth. It is usually needed for the molars at the back of a horse's mouth when they become sharp or uneven.

Rasp (see *Shoeing Tools*)

Ray (see *Markings, Other*)

Rearing (see *Vices*)

Reins (see *Bridle*)

RIBS
A horse has eight true ribs and ten false ones (in pairs). The ribs should be rounded and well sprung.

RINGBONE
A bony formation of the pastern bones which may be above the coronet or below it. It can be hereditary or caused by concussion. Call the vet for special treatment. The horse will be severely lame.

RINGWORM
A skin disease shown by circles where the hair has been pulled away. The cause is a special fungi which grows at the root of the hair. Rings occur mainly on the neck and shoulders The disease is highly contagious (to human as well as horses) so the horse must be isolated. Disinfect stable utensils and treat the patches with iodine. Call the vet. Horses often get ringworm when turned out with infected cattle.

RISEN CLENCH
When a clench on the shoe has risen and sticks out. The shoe may become loose and the blacksmith should be called.

Roan (see *Colours*)

ROARING
This is a noise which can be heard when the horse breathes in. It is most apparent at the gallop. Roaring is due to a damaged larynx which involves the paralysis of one or more nerves in the throat. An operation called hobdaying can be performed to alleviate this condition. This operation is now much more common than the old treatment of tubing where a tube was inserted into the windpipe to provide a clear air intake for the horse. Roaring is more common in large horses than ponies. It can be inherited and is sometimes caused by strangles or can follow an attack of influenza or pneumonia.

ROCK SALT (salt-lick)

Blocks of salt kept for a horse to lick. (Salt is a necessary mineral for a healthy horse.) Can be bought in a block with minerals added.

Roller (see *Clothing*)

Roots (see *Feeds*)

ROUGHING OFF

A term used to describe horses that are turned out to grass after being stabled. The process should be done gradually.

RUB-DOWN

A horse should always be rubbed down with straw or a stable rubber after he has been brought in sweating or wet from the rain.

RUGS

Rugs are generally used to keep a stabled horse warm.

NIGHT RUG. A rug for warmth in the stable, made of jute or hemp and lined with woollen blanketing. One or two blankets may be required under a night rug in very cold weather. It is used with a webbing surcingle or a roller.

DAY RUG. A rug of woollen material for warmth in the stable. Often the owner's initials are sewn on the corner.

NEW ZEALAND RUG. A rug made of waterproof canvas, lined with blanketing, used on ponies out at grass for protection against wind and rain. A surcingle and leg straps are attached. These rugs need watching carefully as they can become dislodged if a pony rolls, etc.

91

RUGS

cotton summer sheet and surcingle

jute night rug and anti-cast roller

anti-sweat rug

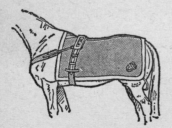

paddock sheet

woollen day rug and roller

new zealand rug

woollen underblanket

SUMMER SHEET. A cotton rug protecting a groomed horse from flies and dust. A fillet string should be attached at the back to prevent the rug from flapping in the wind.

ANTI-SWEAT RUG. A mesh cotton sheet which is used to cool off a hot horse.

RUGGING-UP (putting on). The rug should be gathered up and thrown over the horse's back well towards the front. The front buckle is then fastened and the rug pulled back from behind the horse. The roller is put on and buckled from the near side. It should run under the stomach in the same position as the girth. Smooth down the rug beneath the roller and make sure it is well forward at the shoulders.

OFF-RUGGING (taking off). First unbuckle the roller and remove it. Undo the breast buckle and fold the front part of the rug back. Then, sliding the rug backwards, remove it with the left hand, holding it in the centre at the front and back.

Running Martingale (see *Martingales*)

SADDLE
The saddle assists the rider in sitting comfortably on the horse. It is essential for a saddle to fit well and there should be no pressure on the horse's spine or any weight on the loins. The front arch must be wide and high enough so as not to pinch or press on the withers.

The various parts of the saddle are as follows:

BARS, STIRRUP. A steel bar attached on each side under the skirt on which the stirrups are hung. For safety, always unhinge before riding and keep oiled.

CANTLE. The back of the saddle.

FLAPS, SADDLE. The leather sides of the saddle.

FLAPS, SWEAT. The under flaps which keep sweat from the saddle flaps and, in the case of a half panel, the girth buckles from touching the sides of the horse.

GIRTH STRAPS (Tabs.) The girth is attached to these straps and there are usually three so that if one should break there is a spare.

GULLET. The channel between the two panels which leaves room for the horse's spine.

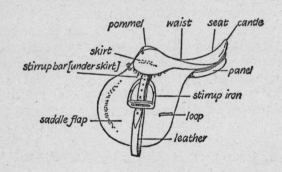

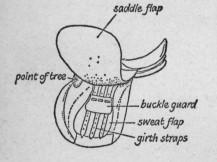

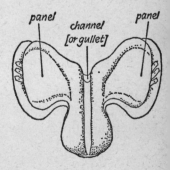

KNEE ROLL. A pad attached to the underside of the saddle flap or to the panel to keep the knee in place. Most commonly found on jumping and general purpose saddles.

PANEL. The panel is stuffed with felt or wool. There are two sorts of panel – half and full. The half panel only reaches halfway down the saddle flap, and there is a larger sweat flap. The rider's legs are thus nearer to the horse. The full panel reaches to the bottom of the saddle flap and only has a short sweat flap.

POMMEL. The front arch of the saddle which covers the front of the tree.

SEAT. The section between the cantle and waist.

SKIRT. A flap of leather which covers the stirrup bar and protects the rider's legs from the bar.

TREE. This is the frame on which the saddle is built. It is made of beech wood. It is very important for the tree to be checked every so often by a saddler because, if a horse is ridden in a saddle with a broken tree, it will injure his back. The tree may easily break if the saddle is dropped or if a horse rolls with his saddle on.

WAIST. The narrow part just below the pommel.

SADDLES, TYPES OF

DRESSAGE SADDLE. A specially designed saddle for the seat required in dressage which places the rider in the centre of the saddle. The seat of the saddle is short and slightly dipped and the flaps are almost straight with only a little knee support.

GENERAL PURPOSE SADDLE. A saddle used for all purposes. It is similar to a jumping saddle but not cut as far forward and often has a spring tree.

95

SADDLES

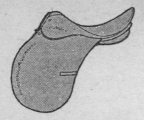

general purpose

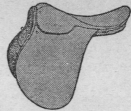

hunting

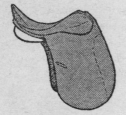

dressage

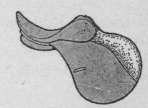

jumping

flat racing

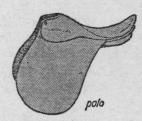

polo

sidesaddle

showing

HUNTING SADDLE. An old type of saddle with only a small dip in the seat and with near-straight flaps. This type is not often used nowadays for hunting as it has been replaced by the general purpose saddle, and many people use jumping saddles.

JUMPING SADDLE. A spring tree saddle with a deep seat. It is forward cut with knee rolls and designed to keep the rider in a forward position for jumping.

PONY SADDLE. This is similar to the hunting saddle but with a slightly deeper seat.

RACING SADDLE. A very small saddle weighing about 2 or 3 lbs. The flaps are cut very far forward to allow for the forward position.

SHOWING SADDLE. This saddle is similar to the hunting saddle but has even straighter flaps in order to show off the horse's front.

SIDE SADDLE. A saddle made for ladies so that they sit with both legs on the same side. Rarely seen nowadays except in showing classes.

SADDLE BRACKET
A wall bracket on which the saddle may be kept in the tack room.

SADDLE CLOTH
A rectangular cloth placed under the saddle usually to keep the lining of the saddle clean or just for smartness.

SADDLE HORSE
A wooden stand on which saddles can be kept and cleaned.

P.C.—D

SADDLE LININGS
The different types of saddle lining are leather, linen and serge. A leather lining is the most efficient and will last for years if the saddle is kept well. Linen is also satisfactory but does not last so long. Serge is hard to keep clean and does not wear well. (see *Tack Cleaning*)

SADDLE SOAP
A soap used for cleaning the saddle with a sponge. Can be bought in a tin or a glycerine bar. (see *Tack Cleaning*)

Saddle Sore (see *Galls*)

Safety Stirrups (see *Stirrups*)

Salt-lick (see *Rock Salt*)

SANDCRACK
The wall of the hoof splits, usually near the coronet, and bleeding sometimes occurs. The cause is often too much fast work on hard ground. For treatment special shoeing is a help and clips can be used to hold the sides of the crack together.

SAUSAGE BOOT

A special ring of leather that can be used as a prevention against a capped elbow. (see *Capped Elbow*)

Sawdust (see *Bedding*)

Seat (see *Saddle*)

Second Thigh (see *Points of the Horse*, *Gaskin*)

SEEDY TOE

A swelling in the horn caused by separation of the crust at the toe. The horse will be lame and a hollow sound heard when the foot is tapped. Cavities inside the horn may develop and should be filled with stockholm tar. Cold applications will bring down swelling. It is advisable to consult a vet.

Serge (see *Saddle Linings*)

Set-fair (see *Grooming*)

Shavings (see *Bedding*)

SHEEPSKIN NOSEBAND

A wide piece of sheepskin covering the noseband at the front. This is often used in racing to encourage a horse to concentrate.

SHELTER

For a pony living at grass all the year round some kind of shelter is needed against wind and rain in winter and flies in summer. The shelter may be a large open shed or just a thick hedge or some large shady trees. But for an open field exposed to much wind, a shed is essential. This should have a wide open front and an earthen or perhaps deep litter floor)

SHOES

Shoes are worn to prevent a horse's hooves cracking and breaking on hard ground when working. Foals should never be shod and horses on holiday should have their shoes removed.

The shoe is basically a bar of iron, usually known as the web, shaped and stamped with nail holes. There are seven of these on an ordinary shoe, three on the inside and four on the outside. The shoe is seated on the bearing surface (slightly hollowed out) and usually fullered on the ground surface (a groove for the nails). Many specially shaped shoes can be made for horses with diseases of the feet such as laminitis, navicular or corns and for horses with ringbone or sidebone. The shoe must be made to fit the foot, not the foot to the shoe.

SHOEING

Shoeing involves the making, fitting, and fixing of the shoe to the horse's foot. A horse should be shod about every 4 weeks depending on how much work he is doing. If the horse is taken to the farrier at his forge and shod there, this is known as hot shoeing because the shoes are fitted while still hot. If the farrier visits the horse at home he can either bring a portable forge or shoe cold. Hot shoeing is preferable because the shoes are likely to fit better.

TO SHOE (so that you know what your blacksmith should be doing). First the old shoes are removed. To do this the clenches are cut and pincers are used for levering off the old shoe. The drawing knife and rasp are then used to prepare the foot for the new shoe. Overgrowth of horn is cut back and the foot is rasped to level it. The new shoe is now fitted and the nails driven in. The ends of the nails are twisted off and the remaining parts turned over to form clenches. The rasp is used to tidy up the wall of the hoof and the clips are hammered into position.

REASONS FOR RESHOEING. The shoe is cast (lost completely) or the shoe may simply become loose. The shoe may show risen clenches which will eventually mean a loose shoe. The toe may have grown too long and be causing the horse to stumble or the wall may be overgrowing the shoe. Lastly, the horse will need reshoeing when the shoe has grown very worn and thin.

Shoe-boil (see *Capped Elbow*)

SHOEING TOOLS

ANVIL. A base of iron used by the blacksmith for shaping the shoe.

BUFFER. A tool used by the blacksmith together with a driving hammer to cut the clenches so the shoes can be removed.

DRAWING KNIFE. (toeing knife). A tool used for cutting back the overgrown wall of the foot and trimming up ragged parts of the sole and frog.

DRIVING HAMMER. A tool used with the buffer to cut the clenches when removing the shoe and for nailing the shoe to the foot.

PINCERS. A tool used to lever the old shoe from the hoof and also to twist off the ends of new nails before they are turned over to make clenches.

PRITCHEL. A tool for carrying a hot shoe from the forge to the foot.

RASP. This tool is used to make a level surface before a new shoe is put on. Then it levels the wall of the foot where the horn and shoe meet and tidies up the clenches.

SHOES, TYPES OF

BAR-SHOE. A specially made shoe with a bar stretching across the heel used on feet that need pressure taken off the heels because of corns, or injured heels.

FEATHER-EDGED SHOE (anti-brushing). A specially adapted shoe to reduce the risk of brushing. The inner side of the shoe has no nails and is thinner in width that the outside of the shoe.

SHOES AND SHOEING TOOLS

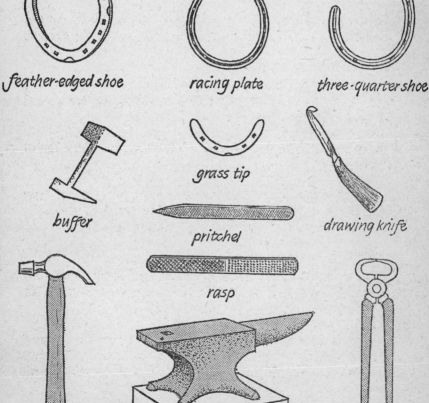

hunter hind shoe [fullered]

bar shoe

plain shoe

feather-edged shoe

racing plate

three-quarter shoe

buffer

grass tip

drawing knife

pritchel

rasp

driving hammer

anvil

pincers

GRASS TIPS. Half-length shoes for horses at grass. The shoes are only used to prevent the wall of the hoof splitting in front.

HUNTER SHOE. The general type of shoe used on hunters and other horses for riding. The shoes are slightly concave for better grip and the ground surface is fullered. The heels are rounded off and usually the hind shoe has a rolled toe, two clips and a calkin on the outside heel and a wedge on the inside.

PLAIN STAMPED SHOE. A simple shoe for horses in slow work. This shoe has a toe clip and. nail holes. It is not fullered.

RACING PLATE. A light shoe used on racehorses.

THREE QUARTER SHOE. The length of this shoe ends before the heels. It helps to prevent corns and capped elbow.

SIDEBONE
A bony growth formed in the heel region. The cause may be hereditary or a result of previous injury. The elasticity of the heels is lost. They can be treated by blistering or with special shoes. Consult a vet.

Singeing (see *Trimming*)

Skip (see *Stable Tools*)

Skirt (see *Saddle*)

SNAFFLES
There are many different varieties of snaffles. The more important are:

104

JOINTED SNAFFLE (ordinary ring). A jointed bit acting on the bars of the mouth and the lips. It is made of metal and has a nutcracker action having a squeezing effect across the lower jaw.

EGGBUT SNAFFLE (jointed). This is also a jointed snaffle but it has specially designed rings to prevent the horse's lips being pinched. It is suitable for most horses.

UNJOINTED SNAFFLE. An unjointed snaffle may be either half-moon or straight bar. It can be made of metal, rubber or vulcanite and is very mild. Suitable for horses afraid of a bit or with injured mouths. Also good for young horses.

TWISTED SNAFFLE. The mouth of this bit has a sharp edge giving a twisted appearance. The bit is very severe and should not be used.

jointed loose ring snaffle

jointed eggbutt snaffle

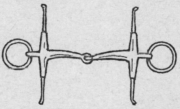

loose ring fulmer snaffle

mullen mouth snaffle

jointed twisted snaffle

Snip (see *Markings, Head*)

Sock (see *Markings, Leg*)

SOLE
This is the covering which protects the underneath of the foot. It should be slightly concave (see *Foot, parts of*)

SPAVIN, BOG
A soft swelling of the ligament on the inside of the hock caused by strain. It should be treated by fomentation.

SPAVIN, BONE
A bony swelling on the inside of the hock just below the joint caused by bad conformation or concussion. The horse will start off lame, dragging its toe, but after exercise lameness will almost disappear. Special treatment, e.g. firing and shoes with wedged heels will be necessary

SPLINT
A small bony swelling on the splint bone usually caused by working a young horse too hard. The horse will be lame while the splint is forming but after six years of age a splint rarely causes lameness. Can be treated by blistering.

Sponge (see *Grooming Tools*)

SPRAINED FETLOCK
A painful swelling at the joint resulting from a twist. Kaolin paste and lead lotion bandages can be applied. But it is best to call a vet.

SPRAINED TENDON
A hot swollen and painful tendon caused by strain—often by galloping through heavy going or by riding too fast on hard ground. It can also be caused by too much work,

106

particularly with a young horse. It can be treated with kaolin paste or lead lotion bandages if mild, but if there is much lameness a vet should be called.

STABLE (loose box)

A building specially made or adapted to house horses, providing warmth and shelter and facilities for feeding, etc. The box should be about 14′ × 12′ (5 × 4 metres) for a horse, or 12′ × 10′ (4 × 3 metres) for a pony. The door (about 4′ wide) should be in two parts, with a top and bottom bolt on the

lower half. The best floors are made of stable bricks, but concrete is also suitable. The floor should slope slightly for drainage. The top part of the door, or a window on the same side as the door, may be left open for ventilation. A ring for tying up is advisable and a manger fixed at breast-level. (see *Bedding*)

107

Stable Rubber (see *Grooming Tools*)

STABLE TOOLS
A wheelbarrow, shovel, fork and broom are all essential for mucking out a stable. A skip (skep) is often used for collecting the droppings.

STALL
A small compartment in which a horse is tied up. The stall is much narrower and smaller than the stable and the horse is unable to move around. He therefore cannot be kept in a stall over long periods. Swinging bail stalls are often used as a temporary measure to accommodate horses.

swinging bail stall

Standing Martingale (see *Martingales*)

Star (see *Markings, Head*)

STIFLE
The stifle is a joint which corresponds to the human knee. Lameness in the stifle may be due to a sprain or to dislocation. Often a stifle simply slips in and out, the hind leg being dragged when the stifle is out. (see *Points of the Horse*)

STIRRUPS
STIRRUP IRON. Usually made of metal, preferably of stainless steel. They must allow $\frac{1}{2}''$ on each side of the rider's foot for safety (see *Tack Cleaning*)

STIRRUP LEATHER. Long leather strap on which the stirrup hangs. They have a buckle at one end which enables you to adjust the length of your stirrup.

RUBBER STIRRUP TREAD. Treads may be used to stop the foot slipping on stirrups that have developed a smooth surface. They are fitted into the bottom of the stirrup.

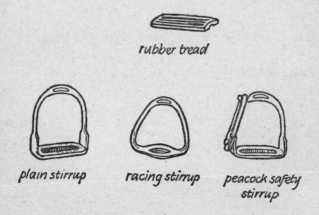

rubber tread

plain stirrup   *racing stirrup*   *peacock safety stirrup*

SAFETY STIRRUPS. Metal stirrups with a rubber band attached on the outside. They prevent a rider being dragged, by coming off if a foot is stuck in the stirrup.

STRANGLES
A highly contagious disease usually affecting young horses. The symptoms are a high temperature, abscesses on the throat between the jaw bones and a cough with the release of nasal catarrh. The horse will be off his feed and find difficulty in swallowing. Stable utensils should be disinfected and the horse should be isolated, kept warm, and encouraged to eat. Fomenting the throat region will help to burst the abscesses. A vet should be called without delay.

Straw (see *Bedding*)

STRINGHALT
A nervous disease affecting muscles in the hind legs causing them to be raised very high and have a stiff jerking action. An unsoundness and an incurable disease.

Stripe (see *Markings, Head*)

STUDS (Frost Nails)
Specially-made nails fixed into shoes to prevent slipping.

Sugar Beet Pulp (see *Feeds*)

Summer Sheet (see *Rugs*)

Surcingle (see *Clothing*)

SWEATING
To dry off a sweating horse, use an anti-sweat rug or straw under a rug – preferably a night rug turned inside out. To

prevent a horse arriving home sweating after strenuous exercise, you should cool him down by walking the last couple of miles.

Sweat Flaps (see *Saddle*)

Sweat Scraper (see *Grooming Tools*)

SWEET ITCH
An irritable complaint affecting mainly mountain and moor-land ponies in the warmer months of the year. The pony rubs hair from the crest, withers and croup, usually against a fence or tree. The pony is generally allergic to something, e.g. spring grasses. There is no real cure but it is a help to keep the pony in the stable and to apply sulphur to the affected parts. A vet should be consulted.

TACK
A term used to describe saddlery and harness. This is valuable and should be kept clean and supple. If left in the damp the leather will crack and break. Being kept in a hot atmosphere will also damage it.

TACK CLEANING
LEATHER. All leather, whether parts of the saddle or bridle, must first be cleaned to remove dirt and grease. A sponge and a bowl of warm water are needed. A knife should never be used on the tack as this may damage it. It is possible to use a small pad of horse hair to remove excess grease. Chamois leather may be used for drying off the saddle. Another sponge or cloth is then used for soaping the saddle and bridle. Saddle soap, either in a tin or a glycerine bar, is usually used; or a saddle grease like Kocholine, but oils such as Flexalan or Hydrolane are also used if the leather is very hard or brittle. The soap preserves the leather and keeps it supple and soft. For cleaning, the saddle should be placed on a saddle

111

horse and the bridle on a special cleaning bracket but a hook will also do.

LININGS. Clean leather linings as for all leather. Linen linings should be cleaned by scrubbing and serge linings by brushing, usually with a dandy brush. Linen linings can be whitened with a whitening liquid.

METAL PARTS. The stirrup irons should be removed and washed as well as the bit. All metal work, including buckles, D's, etc. should be cleaned with metal polish and polished with a duster.

GIRTH. If leather, clean as for all leather. If web, string, or nylon, wash with soap or clean by brushing with a stiff brush.

NUMNAHS. Brush with a dandy brush and wash with soap occasionally. Detergents should not be used on sheepskin numnahs as they will harm the leather.

EQUIPMENT NEEDED FOR TACK CLEANING
Sponges or cloths for washing and soaping the leather
A chamois leather
Saddle soap – in a glycerine bar or tin
Metal polish
A dandy brush
A cloth and duster for cleaning metal work
Buckets or bowls for washing parts of tack
Hooks for hanging tack and a saddle horse for the saddle
A small pointed bit of wood for cleaning holes of stirrup leathers and parts of the bridle

Tail (see *Trimming*)

Tail Bandage (see *Bandages*)

112

Tail Guard (see *Clothing*)

TEETH (see over)
Normally mares have 36 teeth and males have 40 teeth. In each jaw there are front teeth called *incisors* (12 altogether). There are also 12 back teeth called *molars* in each jaw (24 altogether) six on either side. In the male there are four *tushes* which may occasionally be found in mares. When the horse is ONE YEAR old, six unworn milk teeth can be seen in each jaw. At TWO these teeth become worn, and at THREE the two centre milk teeth are replaced by larger permanent teeth. At FOUR the lateral teeth are replaced, and at FIVE the corner milk teeth are shed and replaced. When the horse is SIX it has lost all its milk teeth and is said to have a full mouth. At this stage black cup marks can be seen. By SEVEN a hook appears on the top corner teeth but disappears at EIGHT, by which time the cup marks have become faded and a dark line appears at this stage. From now on it becomes more difficult to tell the age by the teeth. The galvayne groove appears between ten and twenty. As the horse grows older the slope of the teeth becomes more pronounced.

TEMPERATURE
The normal temperature of the horse is 100·5°F. The vet's or an adult's assistance should be used in taking a horse's temperature.

Tendon (see *Points of the Horse, Sprained Tendon*)

TETANUS (lockjaw)
A disease caused by bacteria entering a wound. Symptoms are a rapid increase in temperature, stiffening of the legs and jaw, nervousness and inability to eat. Call the vet immediately. All horses should be given anti-tetanus injections after being wounded, even if the cut is only small. A tetanus toxoid can be given as a prevention lasting several years.

TEETH

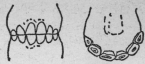

1 YEAR
all milk teeth

2 YEARS
worn milk teeth

3 YEARS
first permanent teeth in centre

4 YEARS
last milk teeth left at corners

5 YEARS
corner milk teeth shed and replaced

6 YEARS
all permanent teeth wearing

7 YEARS
hook appears on corners for one year

8 YEARS
central teeth become more triangular

15 YEARS
Galvayne mark half way down corner teeth
All teeth protrude more

THOROUGH-PIN
A soft swelling found on either side of the hock, caused by strain. The swelling can be pushed from one side of the hock to the other. Treat by rest and massage.

Three Quarter Shoe (see *Shoes, types of*)

Throat Lash (see *Bridle*)

THRUSH
A disease of the cleft of the frog giving off discharge and a foul smell. This is caused by neglect to the feet, i.e. dirty bedding and failure to pick out the feet regularly. Clean out the infected foot, treat by applying dusting powder, and call the vet if the disease persists.

Trace High Clip (see *Clipping*)

TREADS
These are wounds on the coronet either caused by a horse treading on another's coronet or self-inflicted. Treat by cleaning the wound and using a poultice or dusting powder.

Treads (see *Stirrups*)

Tree (see *Saddle*)

TRIMMING
MANE PULLING. This is done to thin and reduce the length of the mane. The longest of the underneath hairs should be pulled out, a few at a time, by winding round a finger or mane comb and then pulling sharply. Scissors should never be used. (see *Hogging* and *Plaiting*)

unpulled mane

pulled mane

TAIL PULLING. This is done at the dock region to improve appearance. Hair underneath should be removed first, working out evenly to each side. Only a few hairs should be pulled out at one time, otherwise a sore tail will result.

BANG TAIL. A tail cut squarely at the bottom just where it reaches the points of the hocks.

SWITCH TAIL. The end of the tail is allowed to grow and hang down naturally.

116

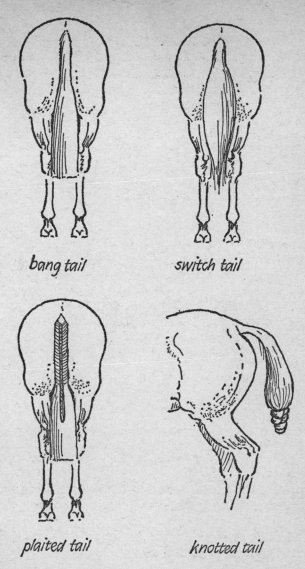

bang tail   switch tail

plaited tail   knotted tail

SINGEING THE COAT. Long untidy 'cat hairs' found on a horse several weeks after clipping can be removed by singeing with a singeing lamp. This requires experience.

TUBBING

A wooden or plastic bucket is filled with hand-hot water and a little disinfectant. The horse's foot is placed in the bucket and water is continually added to keep a constant temperature for about twenty minutes. Tubbing can be used for injuries to the leg and foot.

TUCKED UP

A horse is said to be tucked up when his stomach line runs up sharply, resembling a greyhound's. This often occurs after excessive exertion such as a day's hunting.

TUSHES

These are extra teeth found in the male between the molars and incisors. (see *Teeth*)

TWITCH

This is used to control a difficult horse when administering medicine, etc. A loop of cord attached to a wooden handle is put over the upper lip and twisted until tight. It should never be used on a horse's ear.

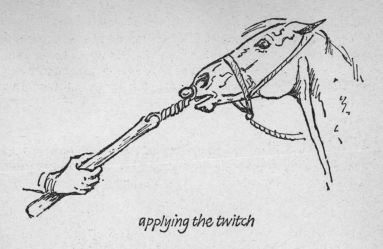

applying the twitch

Veterinary Cabinet (see *Medicine Cupboard*)

VICES
These are bad habits acquired by a horse. Biting and kicking are two of the most common, usually as the result of bad treatment. A kicker should wear a red ribbon when ridden in the company of other horses. Rearing is a dangerous habit, often beginning when a horse is in pain, i.e. from a badly-fitting saddle, painful teeth etc. Bolting is another bad habit which can be caused by fear or pain. Once a horse has been allowed to gallop out of control he is likely to do it again, which can be dangerous. Crib-biting, weaving, and wind sucking are other vices usually acquired as a result of boredom, often due to long periods in the stable. A horse weaves by rocking from side to side lifting first one forefoot and then the other and swaying his head at the same time. One effective method of treatment is to suspend two bricks over the stable door so that the horse bangs his head as he rocks. A horse crib-bites by taking the side of a manger or fence in his teeth and sucking in air. Crib-biters can be recognized by their worn down front teeth. Wind sucking is regarded as an un-

VICES

kicking

rearing

bolting

biting

crib-biting and wind-sucking

cribbing strap

soundness and is similar to crib-biting. The horse sucks in air and swallows it with a gulping sound. Both troubles can be prevented by wearing a muzzle or a special collar except at feeding time. Dung-eating is a rarer habit.

VULCANITE
A material used for the mouthpieces of bits. It is milder than steel but harsher than rubber.

UNDER-REACH
When trotting, the toe of the fore-shoe scrapes the hoof of the hind leg. Special shoeing will prevent this.

Waist (see *Saddle*)

Wall-eye (see *Markings, Head*)

WALL (crust)
This is the crust of the hoof and corresponds to Man's finger and toe nails. On the horse it can be divided into toe, quarters and heel. (see *Foot, parts of* and *Points of the Horse*)

WARBLES
These are caused by the warble fly and are hard lumps, usually in the saddle region. A maggot from the egg of the warble fly hatches out under the skin. Eventually it bores a hole and pops out. (It is dangerous for the maggot to be killed under the skin as it will then not come out). Afterwards, some wound powder should be applied to the hole. It is advisable not to use a saddle when warbles are developing.

Water Brush (see *Grooming Tools*)

WATERING
Always provide a clean and adequate supply of water. It is best to use a water bucket in the stable, or an automatic bowl

system which a horse fills by pressing with his nose. In the field, a clear stream with a gravel bottom provides very good watering. Otherwise, galvanised iron water troughs are suitable. These should have ball-cock apparatus for automatic filling or a fixed tap out of the horse's reach and should be emptied and cleaned regularly. The horse should always be

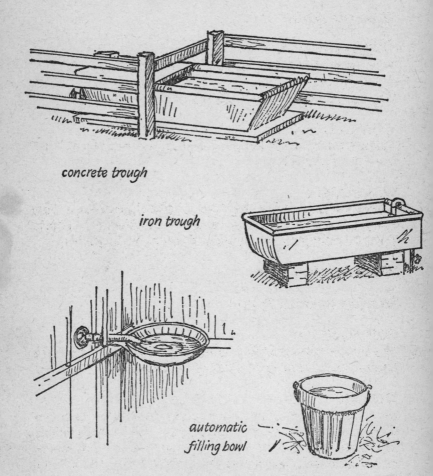

concrete trough

iron trough

automatic
filling bowl

offered a drink before being fed and not be given a long drink just before exercise. A horse drinks approximately 8 gallons of water in 24 hours.

Weaving (see *Vices*)

Weymouth (see *Double Bridle*)

Wheat (see *Feeds*)

WHISTLING
This is a modified form of roaring. (see *Roaring*)

White Face (see *Markings, Head*)

WHITE LINE
This is a white line, round the outside of the sole, of soft horn. (see *Foot, parts of*)

WINDGALL
A soft swelling above the fetlock joint. Lameness is only evident in severe cases. It is caused by strain and overwork. Treat by resting and applying lead lotion bandages.

Windsucking (see *Vices*)

Wisp (see *Grooming Tools*)

WITHERS
The withers are at the base of the crest. The measurement of a horse is taken here. (see *Points of the Horse*)

WORMS
Most horses have some worms inside them and it is only if they have a great number that symptoms will become evident. The horse will begin to lose condition although he may be eating more than the usual amount of food. He will look dull

and have a staring coat. If you suspect your horse of having worms, a worm count can be made by the vet from the horse's droppings and a worm dose prescribed. For a horse out at grass (where he is more likely to obtain worms), dosing three or four times a year is necessary. Various different types of worms are red, tape and lung worms. (see *Ringworm*)

WOUNDS
There are many different kinds of wounds, and most of them require veterinary attention, but a few basic rules should be followed:

If there is bleeding, it must be stopped by applying pressure with a suitable swab, or a tight bandage. All wounds must then be thoroughly cleaned – this is most important because horses are particularly susceptible to tetanus, which can result from a wound becoming infected. If your horse has not already been injected against tetanus, he must be given an anti-tetanus injection. If necessary, the hair must be removed from around the wound – before it is cleaned, to avoid hair getting into it. A gentle trickle from a hosepipe is a good way of cleaning a wound, and this should be continued for about 20 minutes. A weak solution of disinfectant or antispetic should then be applied. Minor wounds heal more quickly if left uncovered, and for any wound that needs a dressing, call the vet. Punctures are the most dangerous type of wound as they can be deep, with only a small opening, and also need veterinary attention. Wounds on the lower part of the leg are more difficult to treat due to the lack of circulation, and great care must be taken in these cases.

YORKSHIRE BOOT
A boot covering the fetlock for protection against brushing.

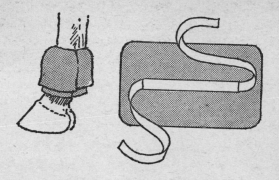

Zebra Marks (see *Markings, Other*)

Good Riding

by Christine Pullein-Thompson

Illustrated by Christine Bousfield

Christine Pullein-Thompson, famous for her popular pony novels, takes you step by step from your first riding lesson to that thrilling first clear round.

With illustrations on every page, *Good Riding* covers mounting, your hands, your seat, the aids, pace and control, schooling, hacking, learning to jump, coping with problems, tack—and more ambitious activities like pony clubbing, hunting, show jumping, gymkhanas, etc.

Learn to ride well, from the very beginning, and discover for yourself the excitement and fun to be found in that very special partnership—a good rider on a well-schooled pony.